BRITISH RAILWAYS

PAST and PRESENT

No 23

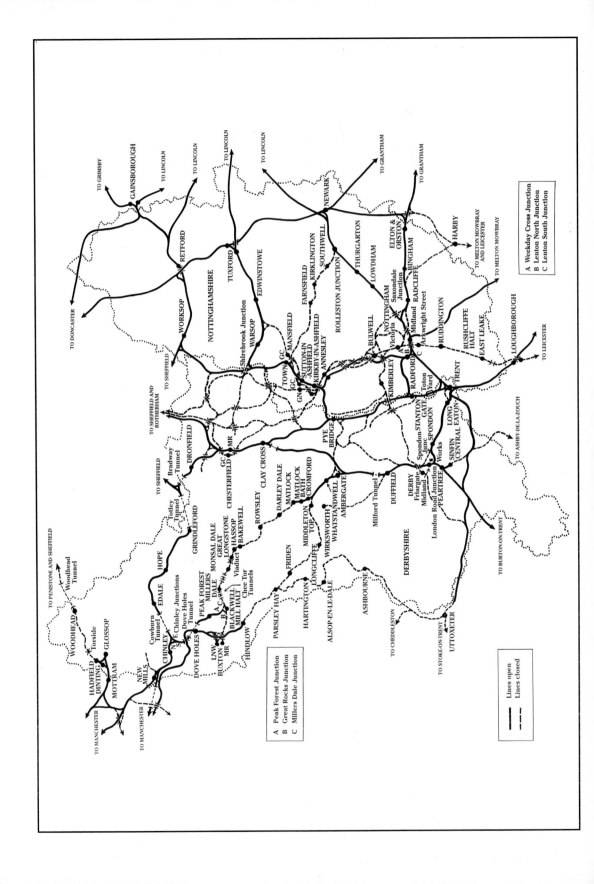

BRITISH RAILWAYS

PAST and PRESENT

No 23
Nottinghamshire and Derbyshire

Chris Banks

Past and
Present

Past & Present Publishing Ltd

NOTTINGHAM MIDLAND: Awaiting departure from platform 2 in August 1958 is Leicester-based Fowler '4MT' 2-6-4T No 42330 on a morning train for the Midland & Great Northern line. The large girder bridge in the background carried the Great Central's London Extension route over the station; it was the opening of Nottingham's Victoria station jointly by the GCR and Great Northern that prompted the Midland to rebuild its station in the city as direct competition in attracting customers away from the Great Central.

On 4 August 1995 single unit Class 153 No 153384, maintained at Tyseley, awaits departure from platform 2 on a Crewe to Skegness working. The girder bridge has gone, removed in the 1980s after remaining unused since closure of the Great Central. Much remains the same at Nottingham Midland, however, giving the station a strong link with the past. *P. H. Groom/Chris Milner*

CONTENTS

First published in March 1996

British Library Cataloguing in Publication Data

A catalogue record for this book is available from the British Library

ISBN 1 85895 051 1

Past & Present Publishing Ltd
Unit 5
Home Farm Close
Church Street
Wadenhoe
Peterborough PE8 5TE
Tel/fax (01832) 720440

Maps drawn by Christina Siviter

Printed and bound in Great Britain

INTRODUCTION

The counties of Derbyshire and Nottinghamshire are as different in character as can be found anywhere in Britain, and yet stand side by side. Nottinghamshire is of a gentler, flatter terrain dominated in the south by its city with its busy shopping centre, university, castle and the famous Trent Bridge cricket ground. In industrial terms, the city means lace, bicycles, leather and textiles, as well as the tobacco industry. To the north-west, stretching towards Derbyshire, is the coalfield belt featured in the novels of D. H. Lawrence, the son of a miner and born at Eastwood in 1885.

Yet Nottinghamshire also has its rural character, along the River Trent, meandering through its heart and creating fertile mixed farming land along its banks. Sherwood Forest, to the west of Nottingham, is of ancient origin and world famous for its association with Robin Hood. In the 12th century the forest stretched northwards from Nottingham for more than 20 miles, but today only small parts survive, the best parts being around Edwinstowe. Then there are attractive small towns dotted around the county: Newark with its ancient ruined castle on the side of the Trent, and Southwell with its magnificent Norman minster. Even the industrial towns have their attractions, such as Worksop with its 14th-century gatehouse and nearby Clumber Park with its many forest walks.

Derbyshire is dominated by its limestone hills and dales, known as the Peak District, much of which is a 540-square-mile National Park. The high ridges of mid-Derbyshire are broken up by some of the most beautiful river valley country in England, especially along the valleys of the rivers Wye, Derwent and Dove. Matlock and Matlock Bath in particular are impressive, set among wooded limestone cliffs threaded by the River Derwent and known as Little Switzerland. Then there is the stunning beauty of the dales, spectacular in autumn, or early spring when the cry of new lambs is heard everywhere - to see these delightful little creatures jumping in the air for the sheer joy of being alive is unforgettable!

Further north is the spa town of Buxton, one of the highest towns in England at 1,007 ft and sheltered by even higher hills surrounding it. At the end of the 18th century the 5th Duke of Devonshire developed the town to rival the fashionable South West town of Bath, and the beautiful crescent buildings in the heart of the town remain as a reminder. Derbyshire also of course has its industrial areas around Chesterfield, Alfreton and Derby itself, but even here there is lush countryside nearby.

When the railway pioneers looked at the counties, it was the attraction of developing the industrial centres and coalfields that decided where to build the lines. Because of the easier landscape, Nottinghamshire was very tempting, attracting the Midland, Great Northern and Great Central. Many lines still exist today, but the closure of the Great Central had the biggest impact on the railway geography in recent years. Derbyshire was dominated by the Midland Railway, as Derby was chosen as the heart of the system with the establishment of the locomotive and carriage works in the town (Derby did not become a city until 1977).

DERBY MIDLAND: The north end of the station on Monday 25 May 1959, with unrebuilt 'Patriot' 4-6-0 No 45519 *Lady Godiva* **leaving with the northbound 'Devonian' for Bradford. This was one of the batch of three 'Patriots' allocated to Bristol Barrow Road for use on this service. Behind the engine is Derby station North signal box, which worked in conjunction with Derby Junction box, situated on the other side of the Derwent river bridge and within sight of the North box.**

  The scene nowadays shows that the semaphore signals and signal box are gone, replaced by the Derby power signal box, which was brought into use on 14 July 1969. Note the redundant loading gauge over the disused track. Second generation DMU No 150012 enters the station with the 13.04 from Matlock on Monday 10 July 1995. *R. C. Riley/Chris Milner*

The works and locomotive sheds were a major source of interest to railway enthusiasts when the annual open days were held, usually in late August. Many a happy memory remains of these events, especially as the visitor was allowed complete access to wander around the roundhouses and yards. There was also the excitement of seeing the latest newly built locomotives on show, as well as ancient stock awaiting scrapping.

The main line of the Midland Railway from Derby through the difficult Peak District to Manchester and the branch to Buxton stand as monuments to the tenacity and courage of the railway builders. Who cannot be moved by the sight of the graceful Monsal Dale Viaduct striding across the River Wye? John Ruskin certainly was, for his unkind criticism concerning its building has been quoted many times. Today it looks perfectly acceptable in its setting and adds to the sheer grandeur of what surely must be one of the most beautiful views in the county.

The closure of this line touched many with sadness, for it was worked day in, day out, by a dedicated team of railwaymen working in often difficult conditions. Seeing at first hand engines toiling away on the long climb from Rowsley to Peak Forest was unforgettable. One could only admire the skills of the enginemen as the steady beat of a hard-working engine echoed around the hills. Yet this line was not given the attention it deserved by railway photographers, but thankfully a dedicated few recorded the action, their work being included here. Much of the trackbed is now walkable as part of the Monsal Trail. To stroll through the limestone hills and dales and see the engineering difficulties and how they were overcome is a humbling experience, tinged with regret that the line no longer exists.

The London & North Western Railway also had a presence in Derbyshire with the remarkable and unique Cromford & High Peak line, as well as the route to Ashbourne. Like the Monsal Trail, both are now dedicated for walkers and are featured in this volume. The only passenger-carrying line now remaining into Buxton is the former LNWR route to Stockport, and this looks set to continue after a possible closure bid did not take place.

The extraction of limestone still forms a major source of traffic for the railways in the area. It was this that prompted railway development in the early years, and will continue for many years to come. The area around Buxton is the place to see heavy trains of modern hopper wagons in action, particularly around Peak Forest where what remains of the Midland main line is used.

The preparation of this volume has not been an easy task, with many difficulties presenting themselves and delaying publication. There were times when completion of the work seemed impossible, but the end result has, I am sure, been worth waiting for. My thanks must go to my fellow photographers Tom Heavyside and Chris Milner in finding the present locations and taking the photographs. The search for material has been exhaustive and the 'past' photographs represent some of the finest work available. My sincere thanks must go to the photographers concerned for permission to use their work, for without their efforts the period when our railways were at their most interesting would not have been recorded.

I hope readers will find the comparisons fascinating and enjoyable, and if you have not sampled the present-day trackbed trails, try them. You will not be disappointed.

Chris Banks
Hinckley

NOTTINGHAMSHIRE

Lines around Nottingham Midland

NOTTINGHAM MIDLAND (1): LMS '4P' Compound 4-4-0 No 40907 and Stanier '5MT' 4-6-0 No 45239 have arrived in platform 3 from Derby in 1956. The railway first reached Nottingham in 1839 when the Midland Counties Railway opened the line from Derby on 30 May. Leicester was reached a year later when the line from Trent Junction came into use. After the MCR formed part of the Midland Railway, a line was opened in August 1846 to Lincoln. The first station at Nottingham, in Carrington Street, soon became inadequate and was closed when a new station with a frontage in Station Street was opened in May 1848. This in turn was completely rebuilt, including a new frontage facing Carrington Street, and officially opened on 17 January 1904. Five through platforms and a bay at the Lincoln end is the layout we see today.

In the view of the station on Friday 4 August 1995 it can be seen that the nearest footbridge, seen in the previous photograph, has now been removed, allowing sight of the station clock tower. Class 156 DMU No 156406 awaits departure from platform 3 on a service for Derby and Birmingham New Street. *R. H. G. Simpson/Chris Milner*

NOTTINGHAM MIDLAND (2): The impressive red terracotta facade of the station is the backdrop for Class 56 No 56016 hauling a westbound tanker train on 5 May 1981. Over to the left is the ex-Midland Railway goods and grain warehouse. This was part of a major remodelling of the goods facilities, and the two-storey building cost £42,815 to build and covered 6,333 sq yds when opened for business on 13 April 1896.

Today the goods warehouse has been demolished and modern industrial and office units built on the site. On Wednesday 7 February 1996 Class 158 DMU No 158848 leaves Nottingham on a morning Norwich to Liverpool Lime Street train. *Both Chris Milner*

NOTTINGHAM MIDLAND (3): Approaching from the Derby direction and passing the goods yard on 17 July 1982 are Class 20s Nos 20072 (D8072) and 20168 (D8168) on a Leicester to Skegness holiday train. In the background is a line of Class 317 electric units stored following a dispute over one-man operation.

The view from the same position on Friday 4 August 1995 shows Class 158 DMU No 158783 on a Cardiff train. The yards closed during the late 1980s and the land was sold and given over to use as an industrial park. *Both Chris Milner*

LENTON SOUTH JUNCTION, a mile west of Nottingham Midland station; the line to Radford curving away to the left. In May 1961 Normanton-based '4F' 0-6-0 No 44458 plods past with a freight destined for the yards at Derby. This 0-6-0 lasted in service at Normanton until November 1965; it was sold to Garnham, Harris & Elton at Chesterfield and cut up in January 1966.

On 7 February 1996 rail traffic in many parts of the country was cancelled due to heavy snowfall. Nottingham escaped the worst of the weather, and at exactly the right time the 11.33 to St Pancras gets away past Lenton Junction with HST power car No 43054 leading and No 43073 bringing up the rear. On the left, waiting to leave with a train of coal for Ratcliffe Power Station, is Class 60 No 60094 *Tryfan*. *J. S. Hancock/Chris Milner*

13

LONG EATON station on Thursday 6 June 1968, with a hybrid DMU formed of two Cravens power cars and a Birmingham RC&W trailer composite, Nos M50788/M59153/M50769, on a Lincoln to Derby working. This station had been opened in 1888 as Sawley Junction, but when Long Eaton station on the Erewash Valley line closed in 1967, it was renamed Long Eaton. New signs proclaiming the name have been placed over the old totems on the platform lamps, but the signal box still says Sawley Junction.

Long Eaton is still an open station and has changed little over the years - even the attractive platform shelters have survived. The old-style signalling and signal box have, however, now been replaced. An unidentified Class 43 HST passes by with a morning St Pancras to Sheffield express on 10 July 1995. *David Percival/Chris Milner*

TOTON YARD is situated in the Erewash Valley at its lowest point, near Stapleford & Sandiacre. By 1884 there were five reception roads and 17 sorting sidings on the down side and nine reception and 16 sorting sidings on the up side. Hump shunting began in 1901, and in 1939 a modernisation of the down yard was completed, resulting in 35 sidings. The up yard modernisation was not completed until 1952 and then comprised four fans of sorting sidings with a total of 37 sidings and 11 arrival lines with 20 storage roads. Nearby Toton depot looked after the needs of the locomotives, as it still does today. This view over the yards from the up side was recorded in 1978 and shows Class 31 diesels Nos 31301 (D5834) and 31311 (D5845) on a coal train working for one of the nearby power stations. Note the now old-fashioned wagons.

In the Yard on 4 August 1995 are Class 58 diesels Nos 58013 and 58025 on 'merry-go-round' (MGR) trains for Ratcliffe Power Station. Some rationalisation of the yards has now taken place and modern wagons have taken over complete-ly from the older examples seen in the previous photograph. *Both Chris Milner*

STANTON GATE sidings are a few miles further north of Toton on the Erewash Valley line. Passenger services over the route were withdrawn on 2 January 1967 and Stanton Gate station closed. This view on Saturday 4 June 1966 shows York-based 'WD' Austerity 2-8-0 No 90078 with a train of northbound empties. This engine transferred to Sunderland four months later, only to be withdrawn the following month.

At Stanton Gate on 4 August 1995 is Class 60 No 60011 *Cader Idris* heading north light engine from Toton and meeting class-mate No 60006 *Great Gable* approaching on an MGR train for Ratcliffe Power Station. The five tracks remain, but the sidings and signal box have now gone. *6201 Princess Elizabeth Society Ltd/Chris Milner*

Lines around Nottingham Victoria

NOTTINGHAM VICTORIA: We return to the heart of Nottingham for this view at the north end of Victoria station on Sunday 18 September 1960. Stanier '5MT' 4-6-0 No 44691, which had been transferred from Neasden to Leicester Central shed the previous June, emerges from Mansfield Road Tunnel and runs into the station with stock for a Marylebone working. As can be seen, the station was situated in a man-made excavation cut out from the sandstone rock. The station was opened on 24 May 1900, a year after the Great Central services from Sheffield to London commenced. The cost of the construction was quoted as being in excess of £1 million.

Through trains from Nottingham Victoria to Marylebone ceased from 5 September 1966 and the station closed completely on 2 September 1967 when at 17.34 the last DMU left for Rugby. By March 1968 the station was completely gone, only the clock tower remaining. The Victoria Shopping Centre now occupies the site, but the area we see in the previous photograph up to the tunnel mouth is now being redeveloped as a new store for the House of Fraser Group, as recorded here on 7 February 1996. *Hugh Ballantyne/ Chris Milner*

WEEKDAY CROSS JUNCTION, in Nottingham city centre, on Friday 30 May 1969, and arriving light engine on the ex-Great Northern line from Grantham is Class 20 diesel No D8168 (20168). Running south to the right of the signal box towards the girder bridge over the Midland station is the ex-Great Central line, carrying passengers no more. After the closure of Victoria station, Arkwright Street was re-opened for the DMU service to Rugby, but this in turn closed on 3 May 1969. For a few more years freight traffic to the MOD depot at Ruddington kept this section open, trains running up from there into the Victoria Street tunnel at Weekday Cross, then reversing up the GN line to Trent Lane Junction and then on to the Midland line. This ceased in April 1974 when a new line to Ruddington was commissioned from the Midland main line at Loughborough.

The blue brick viaduct is still much in evidence at Weekday Cross on 4 August 1995; the archways underneath are now used for the motor trade. *David Percival/Chris Milner*

RUSHCLIFFE HALT, south of Nottingham on the Great Central, was opened in 1911 and had sidings serving the British Gypsum works established there. Stanier '5MT' 4-6-0 No 45342 hurries by on a semi-fast to Leicester in 1964. On the closure of Annesley shed on 14 June 1965, No 45342 was transferred to Carnforth and remained active until the last week of steam traction in August 1968. Its last duty on 3 August was acting as the shunting engine at Barrow-in-Furness.

Underneath the undergrowth at Rushcliffe Halt in July 1995 the track is still in place, hopefully one day to be used again when the preserved Great Central Railway based in Loughborough is extended north. *J. S. Hancock/Chris Milner*

BARNSTON TUNNEL, EAST LEAKE: South of East Leake on the Great Central, near the Nottinghamshire border, is the 100-yards-long Barnston Tunnel. This is the southern portal in September 1959 with an Annesley to Woodford fast freight emerging in the charge of '9F' 2-10-0 No 92010. This locomotive had gone new to March depot in May 1954 and moved on to the Great Central at Annesley in February 1957 along with nine other members of the class, a further 11 following the next month. Here it stayed until March 1963 when it was transferred to Wellingborough. Final withdrawal came in April 1966 from Carlisle Kingmoor.

In July 1995 the trackbed is now covered in undergrowth, but beneath can still be found the track over which No 92010 is running. *P. H. Groom/Chris Milner*

BULWELL NORTH JUNCTION lay north of Nottingham on the Great Central near Bulwell Common station. The view from the Station Road bridge in 1959 shows a 'B1' 4-6-0 and a 'V2' 2-6-2 heading the southbound 'South Yorkshireman'. Leading off to the left behind the signal box is the single 'down' line to Bestwood Junction on the ex-Great Northern Leen Valley route; the 'up' line to Bestwood runs to the right in front of the embankment, obscured by the smoke from the 'V2'.

The whole area is now covered by recently built houses. The blue brick bridge from which this 7 February 1996 view was obtained still stands and now divides the estate into two halves. *J. S. Hancock/Chris Milner*

Nottingham to Newark and the Southwell branch

LOWDHAM: Engineered by George Stephenson for the Midland Railway, the line from Nottingham to Newark opened on 3 August 1846; it had only taken eight months to build as it followed the relatively easy contours of the Trent Valley. Violent storms and torrential rain accompanied the opening ceremony and led to the track subsiding just beyond Lowdham, which resulted in an engine being derailed next day, sadly killing the fireman. This view was recorded on Spring Bank Holiday Monday 27 May 1974 and shows a Class 120 Swindon-built three-car DMU leaving on the 17.17 Nottingham to Lincoln.

On Wednesday 1 February 1995 much remains the same as in the previous photograph. Class 156 DMU No 156405 approaches Lowdham with the 13.52 Lincoln to Coventry. *Michael Mensing/Chris Milner*

THURGARTON is the next station along the line towards Lincoln, and on 27 May 1974 the 15.20 Crewe to Nottingham and onwards to Lincoln runs over the level crossing into the station. The train is formed by another Class 120 DMU based at Derby Etches Park for maintenance, and now withdrawn.

Thurgarton station house still stands and is now a private residence. The station is an unstaffed halt and on Friday 12 January 1996 Class 156 DMU No 156422 runs past at 09.50 on a Coventry to Lincoln working. The upside platform has been removed and resited on the other side of the level crossing. The signal box has also been removed, its position now occupied by a Portacabin. *Michael Mensing/Chris Milner*

ROLLESTON JUNCTION (1): This view of the station on Sunday 4 March 1962 shows a three-car Class 105 Cravens DMU entering on a Lincoln St Marks to Leicester working. Rolleston was the junction for the branch line to Southwell.

On Wednesday 1 February 1995 Rolleston is a junction no more; the station buildings have been demolished and replaced by basic shelters. Class 156 DMU No 156422, Tyseley-based, forms the 12.46 Lincoln to Coventry. *John Spencer Gilks/Chris Milner*

ROLLESTON JUNCTION (2): This is the Southwell branch platform on Saturday 4 April 1959, with the attractive rounded-end station buildings. As the main line had bypassed Southwell, a 2½-mile single-track branch was opened in 1847 from the junction. In April 1871 the branch was extended to Mansfield and the opportunity was taken to rebuild the station at Southwell. The line was doubled in the 1920s but the passenger services from Mansfield ceased from 12 August 1929, leaving only the section from Southwell to Rolleston junction to carry passengers. It was operated on a push-pull basis and the train, usually a tank engine and one coach, gained the name 'The Southwell Paddy'. In this view Midland Railway Johnson '1P' 0-4-4T No 58065, dating back to 1889, awaits departure with the 14.40 to Southwell. This was the last of its class to be working and was based at Lincoln. The only other survivor, No 58086, was in store at Bath Green Park.

The branch closed on 15 June 1959 and No 58065 was placed in store at Lincoln and withdrawn the following October. The branch platform at Rolleston was still there on 1 February 1995, but the station area is overtaken with undergrowth. The lamp standard in the background marks the site of present station.
John Spencer Gilks/Chris Milner

27

SOUTHWELL station at 12.30 on Monday 25 May 1959, with 0-4-4T No 58065 again on duty. The attractive stone-built station building is prominent in the background; when this was built the original wooden building was saved and transferred to Beeston.

The Southwell station site is now occupied by a modern housing estate as this 1 February 1995 view shows, and the station building is now a private house. The 6 miles of trackbed to Farnsfield in the Mansfield direction was purchased by Nottinghamshire County Council and forms a ramblers' path known as the Southwell Trail. Along the route the station houses at Kirklington and Farnsfield still exist as private residences. *Author's collection/Chris Milner*

Great Northern lines through Nottingham

RADCLIFFE: We now turn our attention to the Nottingham to Grantham line, running directly east and opened on 15 July 1850. Built by a company with the impressive name of the Ambergate, Nottingham & Boston & Eastern Junction Railway, it eventually became part of the LNER in 1923. Five miles from Nottingham is Radcliffe station and this view was recorded on Saturday 31 August 1963. Colwick-based 'B1' 4-6-0 No 61188 draws to a stop on a Nottingham Victoria to Skegness working.

On 1 February 1995 the train is again a Skegness service, but now formed by single-unit Class 153 No 153381. This is the 11.00 from Nottingham, which had started at Crewe at 09.18 and will arrive at Skegness at 13.24, not stopping at Radcliffe. The station is nowadays served on weekdays by ten trains out from Nottingham and 14 into the city. *John Spencer Gilks/Chris Milner*

SAXONDALE JUNCTION, between Ratcliffe and Bingham, was where the line to Harby and Melton Mowbray branched off, and was controlled by this impressive set of signals. Thompson 'L1' '4MT' 2-6-4T No 67747 heads the 18.21 Grantham to Nottingham Victoria in 1961. This was a Colwick-based engine after transfer to this Nottingham depot from Gorton in December 1960. There it remained until withdrawn in June 1962.

The view from the same position on 12 January 1996 shows Class 158 DMU No 158859 passing on the 07.53 Norwich to Liverpool to Lime Street service. Evidence of the where the siding used to be can still be seen, and a brick hut remains, hidden behind the locomotive in the 'past' photograph. *Hugh Ballantyne/Chris Milner*

31

BINGHAM is the next station along the line, 8½ miles from Nottingham. Another excursion on 31 August 1963 is in charge of Colwick's 'B1' 4-6-0 No 61177 and is seen starting away with a Nottingham Victoria to Mablethorpe train.

On 1 February 1995 Class 158 DMU No 158857 is working one of the Regional Railways long-distance services, the 08.51 Liverpool Lime Street to Norwich, taking nearly 6 hours for its journey. Noticeable differences from the 1963 view are the new station footbridge and the removal of the siding. *John Spencer Gilks/Chris Milner*

ELTON & ORSTON station is 12½ miles from Nottingham, and on 31 August 1963 another Mablethorpe excursion passes through, this time from Derby Friargate. The motive power is 'B1' 4-6-0 No 61361. Note the waiting room on the platform, with the signs segregating the ladies from the gentlemen.

Class 60 No 60051 *Mary Somerville* passes with an oil tanker train from Langley to Lindsey oil refinery on 1 February 1995. Only two passenger trains each way now stop at the station. *John Spencer Gilks/Chris Milner*

KIMBERLEY: Moving to the eastern side of Nottingham, this is Kimberley station in 1961 with 'L1' 2-6-4T No 67746, another Colwick-based locomotive, preparing to stop with a Derby Friargate to Nottingham Victoria local. This ex-Great Northern Railway line opened through to Derby in April 1878 and was built more for the lucrative coal traffic than passengers. The passenger service ceased on 7 September 1964 and the line finally closed in 1968.

Kimberley station still stands and is now used as the offices of a timber company, Charles Manson & Son Limited. Even the roof barge-boards remain, as can be seen in this July 1995 photograph. *Hugh Ballantyne/Chris Milner*

Sutton and Mansfield

SUTTON-IN-ASHFIELD, just north of the closed ex-Great Central station, on Wednesday 28 September 1966. Class 25 diesel No D7515 (25165) draws vans out of the sidings. This was the line that ran through Mansfield and Tuxford, eventually reaching Lincoln, and was in direct competition with the ex-Midland line in the area. The route closed to passenger traffic on 4 March 1963 and finally went out of use altogether in 1968.

The same location on Friday 4 August 1995 reveals that the cutting has been filled in, but the houses remain, now adorned with television aerials. *Michael Mensing/Chris Milner*

MANSFIELD MPD in 1946, with Stanier '8F' 2-8-0 No 8643, Johnson 0-4-4T No 1350 (BR No 58058) and LT&S 4-4-2T No 2122 (BR No 41940) on view. This four-road brick-built straight shed was opened by the Midland Railway in 1882 and was enlarged by extending the rear in 1891. Situated in the triangle of lines formed by the Southwell, Mansfield Town and Nottingham lines, it maintained an allocation of around 28 locomotives. The depot closed on 11 April 1960 and the crews and complete allocation of 31 engines transferred to Kirkby-in-Ashfield. The final allocation was as follows: Fowler '3MT' 2-6-2Ts Nos 40050 and 40054; Stanier '3MT' 2-6-2Ts Nos 40073, 40079, 40115, 40146, 40156, 40168, 40175 and 40184; Johnson '1F' 0-6-0Ts Nos 41712 and 41844; Fowler '4F' 0-6-0s Nos 43923 and 43972; LMS '4F' 0-6-0s Nos 44252 and 44416; Ivatt '2MT' 2-6-0 No 46501; and Stanier '8F' 2-8-0s Nos 48001, 48088, 48119, 48156, 48219, 48272, 48277, 48282, 48405, 48442, 48541, 48621, 48643 and 48701.

Mansfield shed still stands, but is now surrounded by an extension to the covered area in the yard of an engineering company. The shed hides behind the steel skeleton of the new building in this 7 February 1996 view.
Locomotive Publishing Co/Chris Milner

KIRKBY-IN-ASHFIELD MPD on Sunday 9 August 1964, with Stanier '8F' 2-8-0s Nos 48219 and 48405 in the foreground. The depot opened in 1903 as a three-road brick-built straight shed. The facilities were somewhat inadequate for the fleet of freight locomotives allocated, which was around 60 in the 1950s. Kirkby had to wait until 1958 before any real improvements were carried out, which took the form of the erection of coal and ash plants and a new two-road shed built alongside the original building, and seen in the background in this photograph. Kirkby closed on 3 October 1966, but continued for a few more years as a diesel stabling point. The final allocation of 19 engines, all Stanier '8F' 2-8-0s, was as follows: Nos 48045, 48063, 48069, 48098, 48105, 48119, 48124, 48128, 48142, 48192, 48201, 48282, 48304, 48317, 48342, 48395, 48442, 48492, 48673.

This is the view on 12 January 1996 of the site of Kirkby shed. The whole area is now occupied by industrial units and no evidence that a locomotive shed stood here can now be found. *N. E. Preedy/Chris Milner*

Great Central lines

WARSOP: We move now to Warsop station on the ex-Great Central Shirebrook Junction to Lincoln line via Tuxford. On Saturday 11 July 1964 a Radford to Scarborough excursion passes by in the charge of Stanier '5MT' 4-6-0 No 44962. This was the last summer season for the station as closure came on 7 September 1964.

The station building still remains, behind the photographer and to the right of this 12 January 1996 view. The line is still used as far as Thoresby Colliery, with an infrequent service of coal trains. The platforms are in remarkably good condition considering that they have been out of use for over 30 years. *John Spencer Gilks/Chris Milner*

EDWINSTOWE was the next station along the line towards Lincoln, and also closed to passengers on 7 September 1964. On Saturday 11 August 1962 'K3' Class 2-6-0 No 61826 is the motive power for the 14.11 Skegness to Basford North. This was the last few weeks of activity for No 61826 as it was withdrawn from Colwick shed on 16 September.

The station also remains at Edwinstowe, and is now used as a store by a builders merchant, as seen on 12 January 1996. *John Spencer Gilks/Chris Milner*

TUXFORD NORTH JUNCTION on the East Coast Main Line in May 1961, with 'A1' 4-6-2 No 60126 *Sir Vincent Raven* on a King's Cross to York express. The line off to the right joined the ex-GCR Warsop to Lincoln line, which can be seen in the distance crossing the main line on the bridge. As can be seen, sidings were provided for the interchange of freight traffic between the two lines.

The same viewpoint at Tuxford, bridge No 290 situated 131 miles from King's Cross, on 4 August 1995. Just the up and down main lines exist nowadays, with the added difficulty for photographers of the electrification wires. Class 91 No 91020 provides the power for the 13.10 King's Cross to Leeds.
J. S. Hancock/Chris Milner

WORKSOP is on the ex-Great Central line from Sheffield to Retford; the ex-Midland line to Mansfield branched off west of the station, but lost its passenger services from 12 October 1964. On Monday 3 August 1959 Mansfield-based Stanier 2-6-2T No 40079 is working the 13.28 to its home town.

Worksop is still an open station with regular passenger workings from Sheffield to Lincoln. Freight traffic also plays an important part in the line's revenue, and this 4 August 1995 scene has Class 58 diesel No 58040 *Cottam Power Station* on, appropriately enough, MGR empties from Cottam. *John Spencer Gilks/Chris Milner*

Retford

RETFORD (GC): Retford was the meeting place for the Great Central line to Lincoln and the main Great Northern line. This is the ex-Great Central line, which was opened in 1849 by the Manchester, Sheffield & Lincolnshire Railway. Originally it crossed the GN main line, visible in the background of this photograph, on the level. Austerity '8F' 2-8-0 No 90522, based at Retford, heads east with a freight in September 1963, and is about to pass the Great Central engine shed, which was just behind the photographer on the left. No 90522 remained on allocation at Retford until withdrawn in May 1965.

The view from the footbridge on 12 January 1996 shows Class 144 DMU No 144010 leaving on the 10.46 Sheffield to Lincoln service. Thrumpton signal box remains to control the crossing, and the concrete fencing over to the right is still in evidence. The GC line now passes beneath the East Coast Main Line, having originally crossed on the level, and the low-level station can be seen in the background connected to the main-line station by steps and a lift for luggage.
P. H. Groom/Chris Milner

RETFORD (GN) (1): This is the main line station in 1958. Standing in for a failed 'A4' 'Pacific' is Doncaster's 'V2' 2-6-2 No 60817 speeding south on the through road with 'The Elizabethan', and about to cross the GC line south of the station. Retford was connected direct to London in 1852 when the line from Peterborough was opened.

On 12 January 1996 a Glasgow to King's Cross express rushes through with DVT No 82216 leading and power being provided at the rear by Class 91 No 91018 *Robert Louis Stevenson*. There has been a major re-alignment of the track since 1958, and the original platform 2 is now removed. Northbound trains now stop at the new platform 2 further to the left. The original station building and booking hall still survive and can be seen in the background. *G. W. Sharpe/Chris Milner*

RETFORD (GN) (2): Just north of the station, in August 1960, King's Cross-based 'A3' 4-6-2 No 60109 *Hermit*, fitted with double blast-pipe and chimney, slows for the speed restriction with a southbound express. Forming the backdrop is the large goods warehouse serving the town in an age when many supplies still came by train.

The goods warehouse still stands and retains its wooden awnings. On 12 January 1996 it is used by Tarmac Topmix, with offices available for rent. Passing by is the 11.05 Leeds to King's Cross train. *G. W. Sharpe/Chris Milner*

RETFORD (GN) MPD: Retford had two engine depots, one ex-Great Central and the other ex-Great Northern. Although they were at totally separate locations, under British Railways they were classified as one depot under the code 36E. This is the Great Northern depot, the larger of the two and looked upon as the parent depot. Situated alongside the Great Northern station, it was a brick-built four-road straight shed with turntable. To give an idea of what could be found at the depot, a visit on the Sunday afternoon of 20 October 1957 produced the following engines on shed: 'B1' 4-6-0s Nos 61208, 61212, 61213 and 61231; 'K3' 2-6-0 No 61938; 'O4' 2-8-0s Nos 63637 and 63785; 'O1' 2-8-0 No 63736; 'O2' 2-8-0s Nos 63979 and 63987; 'J6' 0-6-0s Nos 64236 and 64245; 'J11' 0-6-0s Nos 64321 and 64416; 'J39' 0-6-0s Nos 64798, 64893, 64906, 64908 and 64961; 'J69' 0-6-0T No 68508; 'N5' 0-6-2T No 69322; and Standard '9F' 2-10-0 No 92037. This view was recorded on 20 April 1965, and the depot closed the same year on 14 June.

The Great Northern shed still stands, and is part of an industrial and commercial estate. On 12 January 1996 the premises are empty and awaiting a new tenant. *K. C. H. Fairey/Chris Milner*

RETFORD (GC) MPD: The Great Central depot, photographed on 26 May 1963, was situated on the Worksop to Lincoln line east of Retford station and alongside London Road. The shed was a small two-road brick-built structure that had been re-roofed in 1952. Present at the shed on the same day as the visit to the Great Northern premises were the following locomotives: 'O4' 2-8-0s Nos 63581, 63608, 63654, 63655, 63688, 63782, 63905 and 63914; 'O2' 2-8-0s Nos 63924, 63925, 63926, 63976 and 63978; 'J6' 0-6-0 No 64241; 'J11' 0-6-0s Nos 64280, 64283, 64287, 64348, 64385, 64395, 64403, 64421, 64422, 64423 and 64451; 'N5' 0-6-2T No 69283; and Austerity 2-8-0 No 90580. The depot closed in January 1965.

The view from London Road over the site of the GC shed on 12 January 1996 shows that the main shed area is now occupied by an engineering firm. The links with the `past' photograph are the buildings and factory tower in the background. *K. C. H. Fairey/Chris Milner*

DERBYSHIRE

Lines around Derby Midland

DERBY MIDLAND (1): The exterior of the station on Sunday 24 May 1959, with trolley bus lines in evidence. The original station frontage, built by Thomas Jackson of Pimlico, London, dated from 1840, but the facade we see here was the result of major alterations carried out in 1892.

A major rebuild to the frontage was carried out recently, completely modernising the facilities and removing the old buildings. It is pleasing that a link with the past is secured in retaining the title 'Midland' in the station name. This view was recorded on Saturday 4 November 1995. *R. C. Riley/Chris Banks*

DERBY MIDLAND (2): The view into the station from the north end on Saturday 19 August 1961 shows Class 45 diesel No D93 (45057) preparing to leave with the 08.05 Birmingham New Street to Newcastle train. The original station buildings are in the background.

The 10 July 1995 view was taken from where the water column stood in the previous photograph. The original buildings are now demolished as Class 60 No 60023 *The Cheviot* passes through with Grange Junction, Stoke-on-Trent, to Lackenby steel empties. *Michael Mensing/Chris Milner*

DERBY MIDLAND (3): This is the south end of Derby station with, over to the right, the clock tower adorning the administration offices of Derby Locomotive Works. The concrete platform coverings were the result of a station modernisation scheme costing £200,000 which was instigated in 1952 and completed in July 1954. The original all-over roof that was replaced had suffered badly from bombing during the Second World War. In the bay platform on a summer Saturday in August 1979 is a Class 120 DMU on a working to Crewe, while in platform 4 is a Class 31 diesel on a working from the East Coast.

In the view from the same spot on platform 4 on 10 July 1995, the only real difference is the new station lighting. The bay platform is nowadays rarely used, while alongside Class 58 No 58045 awaits a path with a Didcot-bound MGR working. *Both Chris Milner*

DERBY MIDLAND (4): Another study of the south end of the station, this time on Sunday 23 September 1984 with Class 40 diesels Nos 40152 (D352) and 40079 (D279) on the F&W's railtour 'Skirl o' the Pipes' returning to Plymouth from Scotland. The three-day tour had used no fewer than 23 different locomotives, but the highlight was the use of the 40s, provided from Carlisle for a run south over the Settle and Carlisle line. Both locomotives were withdrawn in January 1985 and cut up at Doncaster Works.

In the view from the same vantage point the parcels bay platform is now unused. The date is 10 July 1995 and Class 56 No 56134 *Blyth Power* passes by on a Lackenby to Grange Junction steel billets train. The main difference is the removal of the footbridge linking the station to the Works and diesel stabling point. *Both Chris Milner*

DERBY MIDLAND (5): An evocative scene from the past as one of Derby's last active Compound '4P' 4-4-0s, No 41157, leaves Derby for Nottingham in July 1959. Withdrawal came in May 1960, but the engine had been stored alongside Derby station in the Works sidings from January. Here it remained until November when dispatch to Doncaster Works was actioned, where it was quickly cut up. It was somewhat odd that it was not scrapped at Derby, but perhaps the Derby staff had not the heart to reduce one of their favourite engines to scrap metal.

At the same spot on Saturday 4 November 1995 Class 156 DMU No 156406 sets out on an afternoon working to Birmingham New Street. The large water tank, seen in the background of the previous photograph and a feature of the steam shed, has been removed. *R. C. Riley/Chris Banks*

DERBY MPD occupied a large area to the east and south of the station, alongside the Locomotive Works. The buildings we see here dated from 1890; they housed a twin roundhouse, with no dividing wall, and catered for an allocation of around 140 steam locomotives when this photograph was taken in April 1954. The depot closed to steam in March 1967 and the buildings were demolished in 1969, apart from the offices at the north end, seen in this photograph, which remained in use into the 1980s.

The view over to the site of the steam depot on Saturday 4 November 1995 reveals that a diesel fuelling point is now the only provision for locomotives; servicing for diesel units and HST sets is carried out at the separate Derby Etches Park depot, which had become fully operational in 1960. A new purpose-built staff block now occupies part of the yard, seen on the right of this photograph. *Photomatic/Chris Banks*

56

LONDON ROAD JUNCTION (I): Looking south from Derby on Monday 25 May 1959, the steam locomotive depot is over to the left as Fairburn 2-6-4T No 42053 slowly brings a local train from Spondon round the curve to enter the station. This was a Rowsley-allocated engine at the time and would work a local back to its home territory later in the day.

It was not possible to match the previous photograph exactly as the photographer had used the vantage point of the footbridge to the locomotive sheds, now removed. This was the view on Saturday 4 November 1995 with HST power car No 43072 *Derby Etches Park* on an empty stock set after servicing at the depot. Over to the right is the power signal box, built by E. Wood & Sons Ltd with equipment supplied by the Westinghouse Brake & Signal Co. The original 1969 building had a flat roof, which was a constant source of problems until replaced by the pitched roof we see today. *R. C. Riley/Chris Banks*

LONDON ROAD JUNCTION (2): The main line to Burton and Birmingham is seen in this view southwards from the same footbridge, with London Road bridge crossing the tracks and the carriage works beyond. Over to the left can be seen a stabled DMU standing on the site of the small three-road ex-North Staffordshire Railway engine shed, which closed shortly after the Grouping, its duties going to the Midland shed. Completing the picture is Derby-allocated Fairburn 2-6-4T No 42184 on a transfer freight working on 25 May 1959. This engine had been built at Derby Works in January 1949 and entered traffic at Nottingham. Withdrawal came in December 1966 from Bradford Low Moor.

Saturday 4 November 1995 finds Class 156 DMU No 156405 entering from the Burton direction on a local working. The sidings and extended platform seen in the previous photograph have now gone. *R. C. Riley/Chris Banks*

PEARTREE is 1 mile out from the city centre on the line to Burton and Birmingham, and is the junction for the line to Chellaston and Castle Donington; the latter is still used for passenger services as far as Sinfin Central, served by one passenger working each way in the current timetable. The date of this photograph is Thursday 30 August 1984 and Class 47 diesel No 47456 (D1576) gathers speed on a Newcastle to Penzance working. Rationalisation of track is already apparent in this view.

From the same overbridge on 10 July 1995, with the railway infrastructure little changed from 1984, the most dramatic difference is the disappearance of Ley's factory, replaced by new individual industrial units. Class 150/2 DMU No 150202, and a second unrecorded unit, leave Derby on a Crewe working. *Both Chris Milner*

SPONDON JUNCTION was a mile out from Derby on the main line to Leicester and St Pancras. Stanier '8F' 2-8-0 No 48267 heads towards Derby on the avoiding line with a coal train in January 1963. On the left is Looms scrapyard, with two 'K3' Class 2-6-0s awaiting scrapping, the nearest being No 61907, which had been withdrawn from Colwick depot in September 1962.

In July 1995 a St Pancras to Sheffield working composed of an HST set passes the site of the junction. The lines have been severely rationalised; the junction has been taken out and all trains now go direct to Derby station. The scrapyard continues in business, now dealing with road vehicles. *J. S. Hancock/Chris Milner*

SPONDON station, a little east of the former junction, is 3½ miles from Derby towards Trent Junction, and is served by the Nottingham to Derby service. This was the view from the station footbridge looking towards Derby on Thursday 30 August 1984. Class 20s Nos 20161 (D8161) and 20168 (D8168) haul the 09.07 Burton to Skegness working past the impressive signal box.

Far less interesting is this 10 July 1995 view, with the signal box gone; the crossing is now controlled by train activation and cameras. Passing by is the 10.21 Birmingham to Nottingham service, provided by Class 156 DMU No 156418. *Both Chris Milner*

Midland main line through the Peak

WIRKSWORTH, north of Derby, was served by a short branch from Duffield, opened by the Midland Railway on 1 October 1867. The original plan was to extend this line into the Derwent Valley and eventually to run as far as Rowsley, but this idea was abandoned, and Wirksworth remained the terminus. The passenger service ceased on 16 June 1947 but the line remained operational for freight until the 1980s. Indeed, in May 1985 a branch passenger service was reinstated for the annual well-dressing ceremony. This view at Wirksworth was recorded on Saturday 21 May 1955 with a Gloucestershire Railway Society special in charge of Derby-allocated '2P' 4-4-0 No 40416.

At Wirksworth station site on Wednesday 12 July 1995 there are a few rusty rails and the platform edge is still in place. *Hugh Ballantyne/Chris Milner*

DUFFIELD: Looking north from the A6 road bridge at Duffield on 7 June 1952, Derby-allocated Stanier '5MT' 4-6-0 No 44986, paired with a self-weighing tender, was photographed on a Sheffield to Derby local. The ridge of hills in the background is the first hint of the delights to come, for this marks the beginning of the limestone country, the Peak District. The four tracks at this point merged into two to cut through the hillside by the 855-yard Milford Tunnel, dating back to 1840 when the line was built for the North Midland Railway.

The same spot on 18 November 1995 shows Class 56 diesel No 56109 running light-engine towards Derby. The bed of the two additional tracks can still be seen, and the locomotive is at the same position as No 44986.
E. R. Morten/Chris Banks

Past and Present Colour

Nottinghamshire and Derbyshire

DERBY station, platform 1, in May 1964, with immaculate Stanier '5MT' 4-6-0 No 44918 with the empty coach stock of the Royal Train. The engine is in the later unlined livery after a visit to Crewe Works the previous month. It had also been built at Crewe and entered traffic in December 1945 at Leicester Midland depot. Withdrawal came from Trafford Park in January 1967.

Arriving at platform 1 on Sunday 16 July 1995 is Class '43' HST power car No 43058 on the 09.15 St Pancras to Sheffield. Much remains the same, except for the original station buildings now replaced by a more modern design. *Colour-Rail/Chris Banks*

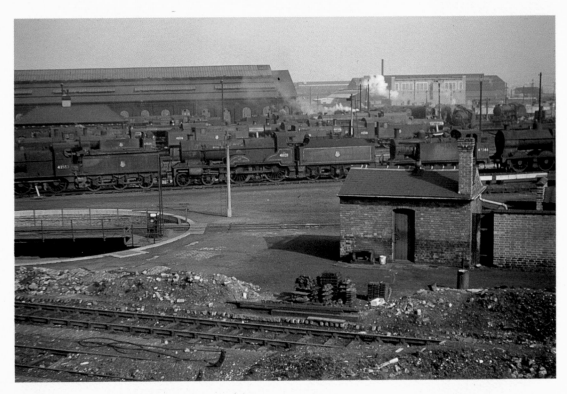

DERBY LOCOMOTIVE SHED YARD in March 1960. This is the view from London Road bridge, which for decades was a favourite place for train-spotters. Centre stage is '4P' Compound 4-4-0 No 41121, which had been in store since withdrawal from the Derby allocation in February 1959. Derby shed closed to steam in March 1967.

The view from London Road bridge on Sunday 16 July 1995 shows only parcels vans Nos 92978 and 92979 to look at. After closure the shed buildings remained in use until demolition in 1969. Over to the left is the Derby power signal box. *F. Hornby, Colour-Rail/Chris Banks*

DUFFIELD (1) is 5 miles north of Derby on the Midland main line, and marks the beginnings of the Peak District hills. Passing St Alkmund's church, half a mile south of Duffield station, is Class '45' No D48 (45038) on what is thought to be the late-running northbound 'Devonian' on Saturday 30 April 1966. The locomotive was withdrawn in June 1985 from Toton depot and cut up at Vic Berry's Leicester yard in October 1986.

The same view from the stone overbridge on Saturday 23 September 1995, as HST power car No 43059 heads north on a St Pancras to Sheffield working. The rationalisation of the track is apparent, as is the growth of lineside foliage, making photography difficult due to the strong shadows. *Michael Mensing/Chris Banks*

DUFFIELD (2): The view north at Duffield from the footbridge seen in the previous photographs. Birkenhead-based Standard '9F' 2-10-0 No 92011 rolls past with southbound empties on Saturday 30 April 1966. This engine had spent most of its existence allocated to Annesley working the fast freight services on the Great Central to Woodford Halse. Withdrawal came in November 1967.

On Saturday 23 September 1995 a Freightliner for Bescot passes the same spot hauled by two Tinsley-based Class '47s', Nos 47297 (D1999) and 47306 *The Sapper* (D1787). *Michael Mensing/Chris Banks*

AMBERGATE JUNCTION on the same afternoon, Saturday 30 April 1966. Green-liveried Class '47' No D1799 (47318) comes off the Sheffield line with an up freight. The line to Matlock and through the Peak to Manchester curves away to the left.

Twenty-two years later, on Sunday 22nd May 1988, an unidentified Class '47' comes off the Sheffield line with a Bristol-bound express. The line to Manchester is no more, being now only a branch to Matlock. *Michael Mensing/Chris Banks*

BUXTON MIDLAND station in August 1962. This station was opened on 1 June 1863 and situated parallel to the LNWR station, separated by the station forecourt. As can be seen, it comprised only a single track with platforms on both sides. LMS '4F' 0-6-0 No 44080, allocated to Rowsley shed, stands in the morning sun awaiting departure with the single coach for Millers Dale to connect with the main line trains to Manchester. No 44080 was withdrawn in July 1964 from Coalville shed.

The Midland station closed on 6 March 1967 and today no trace survives; the site is now part of the car park and road. The ex-LNWR station remains in use, as seen in this view recorded on 16 July 1995. *The late B. Metcalf, Colour-Rail/Chris Banks*

BUXTON STEAM DEPOT in May 1953. This was an LNWR-built, six-road straight shed opened in 1892, and situated alongside the Buxton to Stockport line. It remained open until 4 March 1968 and its last allocation of Stanier '8F' 2-8-0s was transferred to the remaining steam sheds in Manchester.

The depot site is seen in the second view dated Sunday 16 July 1995. The link with the earlier photograph is the line of trees on the hillside in the background. *J. H. Moss, Colour-Rail/Chris Banks*

LENTON SOUTH JUNCTION, west of Nottingham Midland station, in May 1965, with an unusual visitor in the shape of 'O4/8' Class 2-8-0 No 63639 on an eastbound freight. The line curving away to the left is to Radford and Basford Vernon. The 2-8-0 was withdrawn from Colwick shed in December of the same year.

On Saturday 23 September 1995 the junction is controlled from a distant power box, the old Midland box gone. Class '150' DMU No 150132 approaches with the 11.05 Nottingham to Crewe working. *Chris Banks collection/Chris Banks*

MILFORD TUNNEL: The northern end of the tunnel displays an unusual style of portal in the form of a neo-classical arch. Emerging on Tuesday 17 May 1966 is Class 47 diesel No D1825 (47344) on a St Pancras to Manchester express.

Little has changed over the years except for the growth of trees and bushes, now no longer trimmed back. Class 43 HST power car No 43083 leaves the tunnel on Wednesday 12 July 1995 with the 07.30 St Pancras to Sheffield. *Roger Siviter/Chris Milner*

AMBERGATE (1) was the triangular junction for the main lines to Sheffield and Manchester. This is the Manchester line side with Trafford Park-based 'Britannia' 4-6-2 No 70042 *Lord Roberts* running into platform 2 on the St Pancras-bound 'Palatine Express' in 1960. This side of the triangle opened on 1 June 1863, giving easier access from Derby to Rowsley.

All that remains now on this side of Ambergate station is the single-track Matlock branch, serving the original platform 2. The main line through to Manchester closed on 1 July 1968, but the section to Matlock was retained. The station's original buildings were demolished in 1970. On 18 November 1995 Class 150 DMU No 150109 runs in on the Saturdays-only 10.19 from Matlock to Derby. To get the same vantage point from which the previous photograph was taken is not now possible, as the station footbridge has been removed. *Ken Hunt/Chris Banks*

AMBERGATE (2): Running into platform 4 at Ambergate in March 1960 is Saltley's Stanier '5MT' 4-6-0 No 45006 on the 17.26 Sheffield to Derby stopping train. This section of track went out of use in 1968.

From the same viewpoint at Ambergate on 3 March 1995 the connection with the previous photograph is the stone-built houses in the background, hidden behind which runs the present main line to Sheffield. *A. W. Smith/Chris Milner*

WHATSTANDWELL: Just south of Whatstandwell station the line curves round into the Derwent valley and runs parallel with the A6 road and the river. This view is taken from Chase Bridge, which was built over the line in 1883 to replace a level crossing. Stanier '8F' 2-8-0 No 48379 heads north on a Kirkby-in-Ashfield to Rowsley coal train on Saturday 24 May 1952.

Other than the singling of the track, much remains the same on the approach to Whatstandwell. Even the platelayers' hut remains, now hidden by trees and very rusty. On Saturday 18 November 1995 the 13.45 Derby to Matlock service passes by formed of Class 150 DMU No 150109. *E. R. Morten/Chris Banks*

CROMFORD station on Sunday 8 August 1965, looking south, as a six-car DMU set leaves on the 07.20 Buxton-Derby-Lincoln service. The up-side waiting shelter can just be seen beyond the footbridge and was a substantial stone structure of unusual ornate style, with a small tower and tall chimneys. The 'present' view was recorded at Cromford on Friday 3 March 1995 and shows Class 156 DMU No 156411 working the 12.28 Derby to Matlock. The waiting shelter has thankfully been restored, minus the chimneys, which had become unsafe. *Michael Mensing/Chris Milner*

MATLOCK BATH: At the north end of the station on Friday 10 April 1964 Austerity '8F' 2-8-0 No 90157, allocated to Wigan Springs Branch, hauls a southbound train of suburban stock for scrapping. No 90157 itself did not last much longer, for it was withdrawn three months later and left in store at Wigan until March 1965, when it was sold to the Central Wagon Co for scrapping.

At Matlock Bath on 3 March 1995 Class 156 DMU No 156411 is seen again entering with the 15.40 service from Matlock to Derby. The station buildings now house the Whistlestop Countryside Centre, a free exhibition in connection with the Derbyshire Wildlife Trust. The education building holds up to 50 children and can be used for talks or practical work, and adjoining is a wildlife garden and pond. *J. A. Fleming/Chris Milner*

CHURCH LANE CROSSING, DARLEY DALE: On Saturday 14 September 1957 Rowsley-allocated Fowler '4F' 0-6-0 No 44013 heads south towards Darley Dale station on a mixed stopping freight.

By Monday 6 November 1995 the track has become part of the Peak Railway Society Matlock to Buxton project, and its future use for passenger trains is planned. The photograph was taken from the preserved signal box, which in time will control the crossing. *E. R. Morten/Chris Banks*

ROWSLEY (1): Extensive sidings and an engine shed were provided at Rowsley, and this view recorded on Friday 26 August 1966 shows Class 46 diesel No D138 (46001) passing on the 08.45 Nottingham to Manchester Central. Standing on the loop, which ran through the former Rowsley yard, is Stanier '5MT' 4-6-0 No 45190 on a Derby to Gowhole Class 6 freight. The yards had closed on 27 April 1964 and from 3 October 1966 all freight traffic was diverted away from the Peak line in readiness for complete closure.

The same spot on 12 July 1995 shows that nature is taking over. The line of trees in the background is the only link between the two photographs. *Author's collection/Chris Milner*

ROWSLEY (2): Passing the station on Saturday 8 May 1954, a southbound freight heads for the yards in the charge of Stanier '8F' 2-8-0 No 48436, allocated to Royston shed. This was the second station at Rowsley, built when the line was extended to Buxton and officially opened on 30 May 1863. Until then Rowsley had been the terminus of the line, and the original station building of 1849 still stands as a listed structure.

The site of Rowsley station is now a parking area for cars and lorries and, as this view taken on 8 October 1995 shows, the course of the trackbed is partitioned off by a wooden panel fence. *E. R. Morten/Chris Banks*

BAKEWELL (1): In April 1956 Sheffield Millhouses-based LMS Compound '4P' 4-4-0 No 40907 is in charge of a stopping train for Derby. This engine was one of the last four of the type to remain in service, staying at Millhouses until October 1960 when it was dispatched to Doncaster Works for scrapping.

The attractive stone bridge at Bakewell remains in place, as do the platforms under the weeds. The trackbed has been filled in and is now the southern end of the Monsal Trail. This view was recorded on 1 October 1995.
G. W. Sharpe/Chris Banks

BAKEWELL (2): A view of the north end of the station recorded from the signal box in June 1958. Rowsley-based Hughes/Fowler '5MT' 'Crab' 2-6-0 No 42873 works hard on the gradient dragging a heavy loaded north-bound coal train. No 42873 lasted in active service until August 1963, when it was withdrawn at Gorton shed.

Bakewell station building still exists and is now in use as offices; the distinctive chimneys can be seen in this photograph taken in July 1995. The goods yard and cattle pens, once busy on market days, have gone, and the area is now occupied by industrial units. *Hugh Davies/Chris Milner*

BAKEWELL (3); The climb through the Peak started in earnest at Rowsley, and Bakewell was situated on a ruling gradient of 1 in 102, with freight trains being banked in the rear through to Millers Dale and Peak Forest. This is the 'going away' shot of the freight seen in the previous photograph, being banked past Bakewell box by a Midland '4F' 0-6-0.

A ground level view from the same spot on 1 October 1995 shows that the deep cutting on the right is the link with the previous photograph, while the Monsal Trail follows the curvature of the original trackbed. *Hugh Davies/Chris Banks*

HASSOP station was 15 miles north from Ambergate, and had been built at the insistence of the local landowner, the Duke of Devonshire, although it could never have seen much use, as the local population was small in number. It did have a small goods yard which was more successful, serving a much wider area where the stations did not have goods facilities. It was not surprising therefore that the station closed to passengers on 17 August 1942. This view in May 1952 shows Trafford Park-allocated 'Jubilee' 4-6-0 No 45629 *Straits Settlements* passing with an express bound for Manchester Central.

In July 1995 the up-side building is still intact alongside the Monsal Trail, and is now used as the Country Book Store. *E. R. Morten/Chris Milner*

GREAT LONGSTONE was the next station along the Peak route, serving the nearby Longstone villages and Ashford-in-the-Water. No goods yard facilities were provided and the station closed on 10 September 1962. This July 1960 view shows LMS '4F' 0-6-0 No 44117 slowly passing with a northbound freight. This was an unusual member of the class to be found in the area as it was allocated to Rugby depot at the time. It had been transferred there from Bletchley in June 1960 and moved on to Sutton Oak shed at St Helens two months later, from where it was withdrawn in September 1964.

Great Longstone station survives behind the trees on the right of the 'present' photograph, obtained on 8 October 1995, and is now a private residence. Cyclists and walkers now enjoy the Monsal Trail trackbed. *R. H. G. Simpson/Chris Banks*

MONSAL DALE VIADUCT: When this famous viaduct still carried a railway, a '4F' 0-6-0 is seen forging north with a train of wagons on Tuesday 6 August 1963. The River Wye is 80 feet below the trackbed at this point, and the viaduct immediately follows the 533-yard Headstone Tunnel, giving brief but spectacular views into the dale. Engines had a slight respite going north through Headstone Tunnel as the gradient went downhill, but immediately on gaining the viaduct the climbing started again at 1 in 125.

Much remains the same in this 1 October 1995 view of the viaduct, but no more do trains burst from the tunnel and echo around the valley. All is now quiet and walkers can take time to admire the magnificent scenery, as the viaduct is now part of the Monsal Trail. However, ramblers have to make a detour away from the trackbed at this point as the portal to Headstone Tunnel is now sealed due to the deteriorating state of the bore and the rock cutting at the other end. *Author's collection/Chris Banks*

MONSAL DALE (1): A view of the station looking towards Monsal Head on Saturday 24 September 1955. The station opened on 1 September 1866 and the facilities were somewhat basic, the station buildings being of wooden construction, as was the up-side platform seen on the left in this view. No shelter was provided on this side and passengers had to cross the track on a boarded crossing, no footbridge being provided. The station closed on Monday 10 August 1959. Here we see Rowsley-based '4F' 0-6-0 No 44172 heading north on a hopper train. This engine spent many years on Rowsley's allocation, moving to Derby in May 1964, and was then withdrawn during the same month.

The view from the same position on Sunday 1 October 1995 shows that the down platform is still in place, but Monsal Head is now obscured by the growth of trees. *E. R. Morten/Chris Banks*

MONSAL DALE (2): A second look at the station a few yards further north, showing the siding that formed the loading bay. This was used for the delivery of coal and provisions for the scattering of local villages. This scene was recorded on Saturday 19 July 1958 and shows '4F' 0-6-0 No 44241 banking a northbound freight. This was another Rowsley engine and had come to the shed in March 1957 from Liverpool Walton, moving on to Burton in January 1959. Withdrawal from Nottingham came in July 1963 and the engine was cut up at Derby Works the following November.

On 1 October 1995 the view into Monsal Dale is blotted out by the profusion of tree growth; the loading bay has been filled in and is covered in weeds. *E. R. Morten/Chris Banks*

BETWEEN MONSAL DALE AND MILLERS DALE (1) the line threaded two tunnels, Cressbrook and Litton, then emerged on to a ledge high above the dale. Running round the curve from Litton tunnel on a rising gradient of 1 in 100 on Whit Monday 21 May 1956 is Trafford Park-allocated 'Jubilee' 4-6-0 No 45618 *New Hebrides* on the 14.15 St Pancras to Manchester Central. This 'Jubilee' spent most of its British Railways life operating on the Midland main line and ended its career at Burton shed in March 1964. It was stored until October the same year, then broken up at Looms Yard at Spondon.

At the same location on Monday 6 November 1995 the curve of the Monsal Trail and the background hills confirm that this really is the same spot. *Michael Mensing/Chris Banks*

BETWEEN MONSAL DALE AND MILLERS DALE (2): Another scene recorded on 21 May 1956 at the approach to Millers Dale station, just before the track divided into four running lines. The driver of Derby-based Ivatt '2MT' 2-6-0 No 46440 shuts off steam and prepares to stop with the 13.05 Derby to Buxton train. This was a relatively new engine, having entered traffic at Skipton in February 1950 after construction at Crewe. Withdrawal came in March 1967 from Northwich.

On 6 November 1995 the clue to finding the correct position was the stone wall hidden behind the trees, and the surrounding hills. *Michael Mensing/Chris Banks*

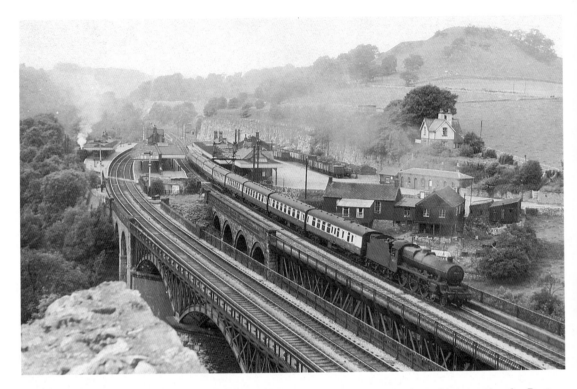

MILLERS DALE (1): We are now 20 miles from Ambergate at Millers Dale, the interchange station for Buxton. On Saturday 30 August 1952 Kentish Town-allocated 'Jubilee' Class 4-6-0 No 45612 *Jamaica* gets away with the 13.45 Manchester Central to St Pancras after stopping at the station. The steam from the engine of the Buxton connecting train can be seen over to the left. Also of note over to the right is the Station Master's house overlooking the station. The layout we see here was a result of a considerable re-arrangement of tracks and buildings that was the answer to serious traffic congestion, and included the erection of the second viaduct and quadrupling of track in 1905. The original viaduct is the one nearest the camera.

The second photograph is the view over Millers Dale station from the same vantage point on Tuesday 15 August 1972, four years after closure.

Finally we see the station site on 1 October 1995 - note how the growth of trees has taken over since 1972. The Monsal Trail now uses the older of the two viaducts, the newer second one being now fenced off at each end, barring access. *E. R. Morten/Michael Mensing/Chris Banks*

MILLERS DALE (2): Newton Heath-based '9F' 2-10-0 No 92077 receives a lot of attention from some of the 280 participants of the RCTS 'East Midlander No 9' railtour during its stop at Millers Dale on Saturday 21 May 1966. This tour had started at Nottingham Midland and made its way to Crewe Works via Burton, Walsall, Wolverhampton and Stafford. After a visit to the Works, the route taken was through Acton Grange, Arpley, Heaton Mersey and Stockport (Tiviot Dale) to reach the Midland main line at New Mills South Junction. Then followed a run over the Peak route back to Nottingham, reached 4½ minutes early. No 92077 was one of the last 2-10-0s to remain in service, being withdrawn in June 1968 from Carnforth.

The quiet of Millers Dale is hardly disturbed on Sunday 8 October 1995. Where the 2-10-0 stood in the previous photograph is now available for walkers, and what remains of the station buildings is used by the Peak Park wardens as a base; toilet facilities and an information centre are maintained for ramblers.
6201 Princess Elizabeth Society Ltd/Chris Banks

MILLERS DALE (3): At the northern end of the station on Friday 18 May 1951 the Buxton auto-train awaits custom over on the right as Standard '5MT' 4-6-0 No 73001 restarts the 16.10 Derby to Manchester Central train. This must have been one of the first workings for this locomotive over the line for it had only been released to traffic new from Derby Works six days previously. It was allocated to Derby and awaits the fitting of the 17A shedplate. It ended its active days in December 1965 allocated to Bath Green Park.

The view from the same spot on 1 October 1995 shows once again that nature is taking over the area beside the Trail. Even the hillside in the background is disappearing under a covering of trees. *E. R. Morten/Chris Banks*

MILLERS DALE (4): Our final view of Millers Dale is this time looking north from the platform end on Sunday 16 August 1959. Stanier '5MT' 4-6-0 No 44846, certainly no credit to its home shed of Kentish Town by the look of its filthy state, heads south on a special. Despite its uncared-for look, it managed to survive into the last year of steam activity, withdrawal coming in January 1968 from Newton Heath.

On 1 October 1995 the platforms are still in place and the rock cutting still overlooks the scene. *E. R. Morten/Chris Banks*

CHEE TOR TUNNELS (1): Northwards from Millers Dale the tracks returned to two to thread the 401 yards of Chee Tor No 1 Tunnel. LMS '4F' 0-6-0 No 44420 emerges from the tunnel on a southbound freight and coasts downhill on Tuesday 1 September 1953. This was a locomotive that spent all its British Railways career operating from Derbyshire depots. From nationalisation day, 1 January 1948, and indeed for some time before, it was allocated to Derby, moving on to Westhouses shed, near Alfreton, in December 1964 until its withdrawal in September 1965.

The tunnel has now been sealed off, as can be seen in this 1 October 1995 view, barring the way for walkers along the trackbed. A detour now has to be made by descending into Chee Dale; the path includes balancing precariously on uneven stepping stones along the edge of the River Wye. *E. R. Morten/Chris Banks*

CHEE TOR TUNNELS (2): When trains emerged from the tunnel they crossed a short single-arch bridge over the River Wye, which was 50 feet below, then immediately entered the 94-yard Chee Tor No 2 Tunnel. This is the view from above the second tunnel on Easter Monday, 2 April 1956, as Stanier '5MT' 4-6-0 No 44859, a Saltley engine, bursts out heading an excursion from Nuneaton to Buxton, and obscures the tunnel mouth with smoke.

Today it is impossible to obtain a satisfactory photograph from the same viewpoint due to the growth of trees. This is the next best thing, a view from the trackbed of the sealed northern portal of Chee Tor No 1 Tunnel on the afternoon of 1 October 1995. Two ramblers descend into Chee Dale to continue their walk to Millers Dale.
Michael Mensing/Chris Banks

CHEE TOR TUNNELS (3): When the line emerged from Chee Tor No 2 Tunnel it ran along a ledge high above the River Wye dominated by high limestone cliffs before entering Rusher Cutting Tunnel, still on a rising gradient of 1 in 101. Leaving Chee Tor No 2 Tunnel on Easter Monday 2 April 1956 is Ivatt '2MT' 2-6-0 No 46440 (seen on page 87 near Millers Dale) with the 13.05 Derby to Buxton service. The distant signals were controlled from Millers Dale Junction signal box, situated on the Buxton side of Rusher Cutting Tunnel, and are giving the road for the Buxton branch.

Chee Tor No 2 and the longer Rusher Cutting tunnels can be still be walked through, rewarding the walker with a fascinating and unique experience. This is the scene on 1 October 1995. *Michael Mensing/Chris Banks*

CHEE TOR TUNNELS (4): Approaching Chee Tor No 2 from the north on Saturday 23 May 1959, running down the grade, is Trafford Park's 'Royal Scot' 4-6-0 No 46122 *Royal Ulster Rifleman* with the 10.25 Manchester Central to St Pancras express. No 46122 had been transferred to Trafford Park from Longsight the week before this photograph was taken, so was a newcomer to the Peak line. However, it didn't last long on Midland line duties for it went back to the West Coast at Carlisle Upperby the following month, to remain there until withdrawn in October 1964.

The 'present' view along the Monsal Trail is seen this time on 12 November 1995. To the left is a sheer drop down into the gorge carved by the River Wye. *Author's collection/Chris Banks*

MILLERS DALE JUNCTION: The parting of the ways at Blackwell Mill with Millers Dale Junction signal box in the background. The line branching away to the right is the branch to Buxton, forming the third side to the triangular junction at this point. Rowsley-based '4F' 0-6-0 No 44429 takes the main line to Peak Forest with a train of cattle trucks on Saturday 6 September 1958. This was another long-serving member of the Rowsley fleet, moving on when the shed closed for a short stay at Burton before finishing at Kirkby-in-Ashfield in May 1965.

Standing in the same position on 1 October 1995, the dividing of the tracks is still recognisable, and the line of hills and limestone outcrop on the left are also linking factors. The trackbed of the former Buxton branch is still walkable to where a bridge crosses the River Wye at the end of Wyedale. Here the Monsal Trail ends. *E. R. Morten/Chris Banks*

PEAK FOREST JUNCTION (1) was at the northern apex of the triangular junction for the Buxton branch, which can be seen coming in from the left. Beyond the signal box is the short 29-yard tunnel. On Wednesday 30 April 1958 'SMT' '5MT' 4-6-0 No 44743, fitted with Caprotti valve gear, heads a Manchester to Nottingham express.

On 8 October 1995 there is no longer a junction here, but a single-track railway still connects Buxton to Peak Forest, now used for infrequent light engine movements and an occasional stone train. *E. R. Morten/Chris Banks*

PEAK FOREST JUNCTION (2): Looking back towards Millers Dale Junction, we see Kentish Town-based 'Jubilee' 4-6-0 No 45615 *Malay States* on a St Pancras to Manchester Central express on Monday 17 August 1959, curving round towards Peak Forest Junction. The Buxton branch can be seen in the background and the River Wye is out of view down in the dale to the right.

On 8 October 1995 the dry stone wall on top of the cutting on the left is in need of repair. The pole carrying the electric cables is a new one and not a re-use of the telegraph pole in the previous photograph. *E. R. Morten/Chris Banks*

BLACKWELL MILL was the third apex of the triangle, on the line to Buxton. The date is Sunday 22 April 1951 and the crew of Nottingham-based Stanier '8F' 2-8-0 No 48279 sit by the trackside waiting for the road with their Gowhole to Buxton freight. Passing Blackwell Mill Halt is Derby's Stanier '5MT' 4-6-0 No 44848 on the 10.30 stopping train from Derby to Buxton. Blackwell Mill was a tiny halt of only one coach length and reputed to be the smallest station served by passenger trains on British Railways. It consisted of two stone-built platforms with no shelters or facilities, and served the Midland Railway cottages situated in the middle of the triangle of lines on the banks of the River Wye. Built in 1866, they are still occupied today.

At Blackwell Mill on 8 October 1995 just the single line to Buxton curves in from Peak Forest. Underneath all the undergrowth the halt platforms can still be found. *E. R. Morten/Chris Banks*

Buxton

BUXTON (MIDLAND) (I): In this view of the bay platform at Buxton Midland, the parallel ex-LNWR station can be seen in the background. Buxton-based Johnson '3F' 0-6-0 No 43329 prepares to leave at 09.30 with the through coach for St Pancras on Tuesday 15 October 1957. The coach will be attached to the 09.00 Manchester Central to St Pancras express at Millers Dale, departing thence at 09.57.

On 8 October 1995 nothing remains of Buxton Midland station, but the ex-LNWR terminus survives. This can be seen in the background with the fanlight window in the station's rear stone wall now preserved. The distant dome of the Devonshire Hospital is the link between the two photographs. *E. R. Morten/Chris Banks*

BUXTON (MIDLAND) (2): Approaching the station is an unusual visitor in the shape of unrebuilt 'Patriot' 4-6-0 No 45507 *Royal Tank Corps*, allocated to Carlisle Upperby, with a train from Derby on Monday 6 July 1959. Withdrawal for this locomotive came in October 1962 from Lancaster shed.

In the view from the same position as the previous photograph on 8 October 1995, the houses and the railway viaduct, which carries the line to Hindlow, are the connecting features. The Midland engine shed at Buxton, opened in 1863, occupied the site over to the right, but this was closed on 19 August 1935 and demolished very soon afterwards. *E. R. Morten/Chris Banks*

BUXTON MIDLAND (3): Inside the station on Saturday 23 September 1961. A two-car Gloucester RC&W diesel set, introduced in 1957, rests in the single-track platform after arrival with the 12.05 from Millers Dale. The lamp has been placed at the rear in readiness for the return run. The Millers Dale to Buxton service went over to diesel operation from Monday 7 October 1957, resulting in the regular steam engine, Johnson 0-4-4T No 58083, being withdrawn.

Buxton Midland finally closed, along with Millers Dale and Blackwell Mill, on Monday 6 March 1967. As can be seen from the 8 October 1995 view, the position of the station is now a busy road. *Michael Mensing/Chris Banks*

BUXTON (LNWR): The approach to Buxton ex-LNWR station on Wednesday 17 September 1980. A Class 104 Birmingham RC&W DMU set, with M50420 leading, arrives from Manchester. Over to the left is the diesel depot, opened in the late 1950s to cater for the new diesel units in the area. On shed is Class 40 No 40135 (D335) and Class 45 No 45056 (D91).

Not a great deal has changed over the intervening years, except that the depot now looks less busy due to the withdrawal of the first generation DMUs. It is, however, still used for refuelling and light maintenance of the locomotives used on the local stone traffic, while the diesel units working the hourly service to Stockport and further afield are now maintained elsewhere. This Wednesday 12 July 1995 view shows Class 156 DMU No 156427, maintained at Newton Heath, arriving with the 09.27 from Blackpool North. *Tom Heavyside/Chris Milner*

BUXTON DIESEL DEPOT: A closer look at the depot on 17 September 1980. Class 40 diesel No 40135 was allocated to Manchester Longsight at the time and was withdrawn from normal service on 22 January 1985. It was then transferred to departmental stock and renumbered 97406. This ensured the locomotive's survival after many of the rest of the class had been withdrawn, and enabled transfer into preservation as D335. It can now be found at the East Lancs Railway, in its original green livery.

At Buxton depot on Wednesday 22 November 1995 is Class 37 No 37108 (D6808), maintained at Crewe diesel depot. Only one other locomotive was present, No 37415 (D6977). The main differences from 1980 are the replacement of the yard lights by a much higher example, and the removal of the siding on which the DMU set stood. Note also the removal of the spikes on top of the fencing to comply with current Health & Safety requirements. *Both Tom Heavyside*

BUXTON (LNWR) MPD (1): After leaving Buxton station the ex-LNWR line to Stockport ran past the steam depot, seen over to the left of this view, and the freight yards. Backing out on to the main line on Saturday 23 September 1961 is Buxton-based Stanier '8F' 2-8-0 No 48712 with a freight destined for Manchester.

The view from the same footbridge vantage point on a very damp and misty Sunday 12 November 1995 confirms that the yards closed in the 1970s, although a few sidings are intact over to the left. The motive power depot yard is now overgrown with trees. Leaving on the 08.40 departure to Guide Bridge and tackling the stiff climb to Dove Holes is preserved Stanier '8F' 2-8-0 No 48151. This was the first steam passenger working out of Buxton for over 25 years and was arranged to celebrate the launch of the new Manchester & High Peak Railway Company, a founder member of the Community Railways Scheme. A second round

trip left Buxton in the afternoon. On the Saturday the '8F' had worked a hopper train to Tunstead quarry, marking the coming withdrawal of the vacuum-fitted double-bogie hoppers with new air-braked wagons, and had been suitably streaked and stained by limestone dust for the event. *Michael Mensing/Chris Banks*

BUXTON (LNWR) DEPOT (2): Buxton steam depot opened in 1892, replacing a smaller shed situated where the present diesel depot is located. Visible in this view on the afternoon of Sunday 2 May 1954 is LMS '4F' 0-6-0 No 44382, with a tender cab, Johnson '3F' 0-6-0 No 43273, visiting from Rowsley, and LNWR '7F' 0-8-0 No 49387. The allocation on this date consisted of 47 locomotives, as follows: Johnson/Fowler '2P' 4-4-0s Nos 40433 and 40536; LMS '2P' 4-4-0s Nos 40655 and 40692; Stanier '2P' 0-4-4T No 41905; Fowler '4MT' 2-6-4Ts Nos 42306, 42315, 42365, 42366, 42367, 42368, 42370 and 42371; Hughes/Fowler '5MT' 2-6-0s Nos 42942 and 42943; Johnson '3F' 0-6-0s Nos 43268, 43274, 43278, 43300 and 43387; Fowler '4F' 0-6-0 No 43842; LMS '4F' 0-6-0s Nos 44339 and 44382; Stanier '8F' 2-8-0s Nos 48166, 48268, 48278, 48322, 48326, 48421, 48451, 48465, 48519, 48712, 48734, 48740, 48742, 48745, 48746 and 48749; LNWR '7F' 0-8-0s Nos 49057, 49132, 49210, 49214, 49348 and 49387; and Johnson '1P' 0-4-4Ts Nos 58083 and 58084. A few weeks before closure on 16 February 1968, 'on shed' were 2-8-0s Nos 48191, 48319, 48424, 48442, 48471, 48532 and 48775, and withdrawn examples 48190, 48336. The last working day for the shed was 3 March 1968 and at 15.40 No 48775 left light engine, followed by 48744, leaving 48336, 48424 and 48442 dumped awaiting scrap.

At the former Buxton shed yard on 8 October 1995 two snowploughs occupy the sidings that remain. This part is free from undergrowth, but the rest of the site is thickly covered with trees and bushes. There was a

plan to re-roof and retain the shed buildings and use them as a stabling point for diesels, but this was not proceeded with. Today that would have been useful, as the present diesel depot is not big enough to accommodate the weekend gathering of locomotives now having to be stabled some distance away at Peak Forest. *K. C. H. Fairey/Chris Banks*

112

LNWR lines and the Cromford & High Peak

PARSLEY HAY: The station and exchange sidings were located on the Buxton to Ashbourne line, and are seen here on Saturday 2 October 1954, with Buxton's LNWR '7F' 0-8-0 No 49348 carrying out its shunting duties. The line, built by the LNWR, opened for passenger services to Parsley Hay on 1 June 1894 and on to Ashbourne on 3 August 1899. The section from Buxton to Parsley Hay was double track, but onwards to Ashbourne remained single. Just south of Parsley Hay the Cromford & High Peak Line joined the route, and this produced traffic for sorting and weighing at Parsley Hay. The line closed to passenger traffic on 1 November 1954, but continued to be used by excursion traffic to Buxton. It closed completely in October 1963, but the connection to the C&HP remained in use until September 1967. The section from Buxton to the limestone quarries at Hindlow is still in use.

When the line closed the Peak Park Joint Planning Board and Derbyshire County Council purchased the 12 miles of trackbed from Ashbourne to Hartington, and in 1971 the section to Parsley Hay, together with the whole of the Cromford & High Peak line. The Ashbourne route is now known as the Tissington Trail, taking its name from a local village served by the line and famous for its annual well-dressing ceremonies carried out on Ascension Day in thanks for the continuing flow of spring water. The 1 October 1995 view at Parsley Hay has the stone bridge parapet as the link with the previous photograph. Behind the trees is the local Ranger Centre and cycle hire shop for those wishing to ride along the trail. No trace of the station now remains. *E. R. Morten/Chris Banks*

ALSOP-EN-LE-DALE station was halfway between Parsley Hay and Ashbourne. In June 1957 Burton-based LMS '4F' 0-6-0 No 44528 and Standard '4MT' 4-6-0 No 75056, new from Swindon Works four months earlier and allocated to Nottingham, await departure on a special to Buxton from the Midlands.

Seen on a beautiful autumn day, 6 November 1995, the line at Alsop-en-le-Dale now forms part of the Tissington Trail, and the site of the station is now a car park for ramblers. The link with the previous photograph is the dry stone walls and line of trees. *Photomatic/Chris Banks*

We now turn our attention to the Cromford & High Peak Railway. The line opened from Cromford Canal to Hurdlow on 29 May 1830, and on to Whaley Bridge on 6 July 1831, 33 miles of single track. It included several inclines of extreme severity and was first worked by horse-drawn trains rope-hauled up the inclines by stationery winding gear. When locomotives started operating, Hopton incline at 1 in 14 became the steepest adhesion-worked gradient in Britain. The line was taken over by the LNWR on a leasing basis from December 1860, then owned outright from 1 July 1887. It finally closed from 21 November 1967, even though it had not been used since earlier in the year.

FRIDEN, C&HPR (1): Travelling south from Parsley Hay we come to Friden, the farthest point along the C&HP that larger main-line locomotives could venture from the Ashbourne line. Here a brickworks produced revenue for the line. It is Saturday 21 May 1955 and a Gloucestershire Railway Society special (seen earlier on page 63

at Wirksworth) has arrived at Friden to take water before setting off to Parsley Hay. The motive power is two of the North London Railway '2F' 0-6-0Ts introduced in 1879, Nos 58850 and 58856. No 58850 was the last of the class to remain active and was withdrawn in September 1960. It was then placed in long-term storage and is now preserved on the Bluebell Railway at Sheffield Park.

On 1 October 1995 the trackbed at Friden is now part of the High Peak Trail, and the site of the loading platform is a car park and picnic area. *Hugh Ballantyne/Chris Banks*

FRIDEN, C&HPR (2): About a mile south of Friden the line crossed the A5012 Cromford to Newhaven road on a level crossing. This view on Friday 20 May 1966 shows Class 'J94' '4F' 0-6-0ST No 68006 on empties for Middleton. This was the final class of steam locomotives to work the line; the first one, No 68030, arrived on 10 April 1956 from Bidston for trials. The distribution of the regular locomotives working the line on this date was as follows: Cromford, Deeley 0-4-0T No 41536; Sheep Pasture, Kitson 0-4-0ST No 47000; Middleton Top, NLR 0-6-0Ts Nos 58850 and 58856, with a spare at Rowsley, No 58860. The trial was a success and 'J94' No 68030 returned in August 1956 together with two others, Nos 68006 and 68013.

The crossing of the A5012 on 1 October 1995 is now only taken by cyclists and ramblers on the High Peak Trail. The farm road remains at this bleak spot high in the hills, but Newhaven Farm Cottage has now gone, a copse of trees taking over the site. *Roger Siviter/Chris Banks*

118

LONGCLIFFE: Another view of the Gloucestershire Railway Society special on 21 May 1955. This is Longcliffe, where a quarry provided traffic for the line, and where a raised siding was provided with ancient water tenders; NLR 0-6-0T No 58856 takes refreshment before heading north. The raised siding is still in place on 8 October 1995, but no longer provides water for the hard-working locomotives. *Hugh Ballantyne/Chris Banks*

HOPTON TUNNEL: A last day enthusiasts' special on the Cromford & High Peak line on Sunday 30 April 1967 is seen climbing between Middleton Top and Hopton, and is about to enter the 113-yard Hopton Tunnel with 'J94' 0-6-0STs Nos 68006 and 68012 in charge. In the background is Middleton Quarry, which at one time was served by a connecting line.

On 8 October 1995 the view from the top of Hopton Tunnel has changed somewhat, with the old railway cutting in deep shadow due to the profusion of tree growth. The trackbed can just be discerned over to the right with a cyclist coming into the sunlight. The poles carrying the electric cables are still there, but Middleton quarry is closed and its associated buildings gone. *Roger Siviter/Chris Banks*

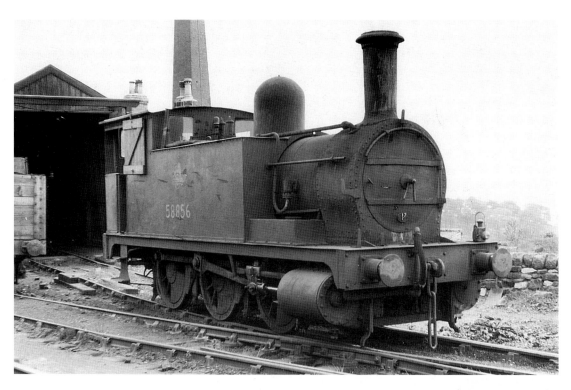

MIDDLETON TOP sub-shed in May 1956. The chimney in the background is part of the building housing the large beam engine that hauled wagons up the 1 in 8¼ Middleton Incline from Sheep Pasture. Standing outside the single-road shed is NLR 0-6-0T No 58856, which was withdrawn in October 1957 and later cut up. Note the wooden shutter on the cab side, which would no doubt have been a welcome home-made improvement in the exposed countryside in winter.

Middleton Top on 8 October 1995 is now a visitors' centre with picnic area, toilets, bookshop and cycle hire point with around 60 cycles available. On a good day all are used, such is the demand to ride along the High Peak Trail. The winding house has been restored and the beam engine preserved, and a signal is also in place, as is a Midland Railway wagon on a plinth. *G. W. Sharpe/Chris Banks*

North from Peak Forest

GREAT ROCKS JUNCTION (1): On Friday 23 July 1976 Class 25 diesel No 25138 (D5288) heads north on a loaded Tunstead to Northwich working and passes the flat-roofed signal box and part of the ICI works and quarry. Banking assistance is provided by another 25, No 25051 (D5201).

Nineteen years later and surprisingly very little has changed at Great Rocks Junction, except for the locomotives. National Power-owned Class 59/2 No 59201 *Vale of York* pulls out from the siding on a Tunstead to Drax working on 22 November 1995. *Both Tom Heavyside*

GREAT ROCKS JUNCTION (1): Looking in the opposite direction north towards Peak Forest from the road bridge at Great Rocks Junction on 23 July 1976, Class 40 diesel No 40128 (D328) is seen hauling a coal train for Buxton, while on the left Class 46 No 46040 (D177) waits to enter Tunstead Quarry. Both locomotives are now a memory, the 40 being withdrawn in September 1982 and the 46 in December 1980. Over to the right a turntable and sidings were once provided, but these were removed in the early 1970s.

The same viewpoint on 22 November 1995 shows Class 60 No 60005 *Skiddaw*, Cardiff-based for heavy maintenance, having just run round its train after bringing it out from the quarry; it will now head for Hindlow. *Both Tom Heavyside*

PEAK FOREST (1): In the 18th century the village of Peak Forest was known as the Gretna Green of Derbyshire, for it was here that eloping couples could be married by virtue of a royal grant, and in one year over a hundred marriages took place. On Friday 18 June 1965 'Jubilee' 4-6-0 No 45705 *Seahorse* is working the 08.00 Buxton to Manchester Central. This was one of the last steam-hauled passenger workings in the area at the time, and *Seahorse* was a regular performer, returning on the 17.22 to Buxton after spending the day on Trafford Park shed. Before being transferred to Newton Heath in June 1964, it had spent many years at Farnley Junction and Blackpool depots. Transfer to Trafford Park was actioned, but not officially recorded, in 1965, and withdrawal came in late October the same year.

Thirty years later, on Wednesday 12 July 1995, Class 60 No 60058 *John Howard* heads out of the sidings with a train of RMC Roadstone hoppers for Bletchley. The station had closed on 6 March 1967, but the down-side buildings have been retained for continued use by railway staff. *Author's collection/Chris Milner*

PEAK FOREST (2): Just a little north of the station, on the other side of the stone bridge that gave access to the platforms, are the limestone quarries. This view on Tuesday 17 June 1958 shows 'Britannia' 4-6-2 No 70014 *Iron Duke*, maintained by Trafford Park, on an afternoon Manchester Central to St Pancras express.

Class 60 No 60095 *Crib Goch* draws past the quarries on 12 July 1995 with empties from Washwood Heath. Fewer sidings now remain, but extraction of limestone continues. *E. R. Morten/Chris Milner*

PEAK FOREST (3): This is the view of the quarries from the other end of the overbridge. The date is Saturday 8 April 1989 and Class 37s Nos 37676 (D6826) and 37687 (D6831) head a rake of empty old-type hopper wagons on a Northwich to Tunstead working.

Six years later, on 22 November 1995, Class 60 No 60066 *John Logie Baird* passes an 08 diesel shunter at the same spot with a train of modern empty hoppers from Salford Hope Street to Tunstead. Note the removal of the telegraph poles. The rear of the train is in the cutting that marks the summit of the line at 985 feet above sea level. A little beyond is Dove Holes Tunnel, 1 mile 1,224 yards in length, piercing the 1,250-foot-high range of Pennine Hills called Cow Low. *Both Tom Heavyside*

DOVE HOLES station is on the ex-LNWR Buxton to Stockport line, which crossed over the Midland Peak Forest line above Dove Holes Tunnel. On Sunday 7 October 1951 Stanier '8F' 2-8-0 No 48558, belonging to Widnes depot, enters the station on a train of wooden-bodied ICI lime wagons. No 48558 lasted in service until 9 October 1965, when it was withdrawn from Rose Grove.

Dove Holes is still an open station and this 12 July 1995 view shows the 17.23 Manchester Piccadilly to Buxton about to stop for custom. The train is composed of two Class 101 units, 101682 (53256 + 51505) and 101681 (51228 + 51506). *E. R. Morten/Chris Milner*

CHINLEY: The Midland Railway's line from Peak Forest, through Chinley and on to New Mills and Manchester, opened on 1 February 1867. It had been completed in October 1866, but had been badly affected by a major landslip at Bugsworth, south of New Mills, shortly after opening. On Whit Monday, 21 May 1956, Sheffield Millhouses-allocated LMS Compound '4P' 4-4-0 No 41062 has just arrived at platform 1 with the 10.50 from Manchester Central, and prepares to draw out to an adjacent platform to form the 12.25 to Sheffield Midland, along the Hope Valley line. When the latter route opened for goods traffic on 6 November 1893 and passenger trains on 13 May 1894, Chinley became a busy junction station. The track was quadrupled to cope with the increased traffic, resulting in a new station being built and opened in June 1902 a little further west than the original. It had five through platforms and a bay at one end for Buxton, Derby and Sheffield locals. Enlarged goods facilities were also provided.

Chinley is now no more than an island platform with 'bus shelter' accommodation for waiting passengers, as confirmed by this Saturday 4 November 1995 view from the former platform 2, which has now been extended over the former trackbed. A link with the previous photograph is the footbridge in the background, as Longsight-maintained Class 101 DMU No 101665 (51429 + 54393) prepares to stop with the 07.33 Manchester airport to Sheffield working.
Michael Mensing/Tom Heavyside

CHINLEY NORTH JUNCTION on Friday 23 July 1976, with Class 46 diesel No 46013 (D150) on a Northwich to Tunstead hopper train. Introduced in December 1961 and first allocated to Derby, No 46013 was withdrawn in August 1980 from Plymouth Laira and finally cut up at BREL Swindon in April 1985.

By 4 November 1995 track rationalisation is evident, together with the removal of the old semaphore signals. Links with the previous photograph are the electric cable pole on the left and the Crown & Mitre pub on the right. Class 158 DMU No 158861 heads home to its Norwich base on the 07.49 from Liverpool Lime Street. *Both Tom Heavyside*

NEW MILLS SOUTH JUNCTION, west of Chinley, on Friday 12 October 1956. The line to Hazel Grove and Old Trafford continues straight ahead past the signal box into the mist, while the line to Manchester via Marple curves away to the right. Bolton-allocated 'WD' '8F' 2-8-0 No 90316 heads away with a freight for Gowhole Sidings. No 90316 finished its days at Colwick shed, being withdrawn in December 1965 and cut up at Drapers Yard, Hull, in April 1966.

At the same location on 12 July 1995 the signal box is still in position, but has far less work to do. The 17.11 Manchester Piccadilly to Sheffield passes by formed of a Class 101 DMU set No 101835 (51432 + 51498). *Norman Preedy/Chris Milner*

Hope Valley line

EDALE: We now turn our attention to the Hope Valley route, travelling east from Chinley. This is Edale station on Saturday 3 October 1959, with a lengthy train of eastbound coal empties trundling through in the charge of an unusually clean 'WD' '8F' 2-8-0, No 90055, based at Staveley GC depot. Withdrawal came for this engine from Immingham in March 1965.

On 12 July 1995 Class 158 DMU No 158761 forms the 12.57 Liverpool Lime Street to Norwich service. The platform has now been shortened for public use and the station buildings replaced by modern 'bus shelters', but the signal box remains in use as a link with the past. Radiating away from the station are delightful walks much frequented by ramblers and giving spectacular views over the vale of Edale and the Hope Valley. *Michael Mensing/Chris Milner*

HOPE is the next station along the route to Sheffield and can be seen in the background of this view recorded on Monday 16 May 1966. Class 31 diesel No D5850, introduced in July 1962 and allocated new to Tinsley, departs with a Manchester Piccadilly to Sheffield local. The waste ground is where sidings used to exist. No D5850 is now allocated to Bescot as 31546 and is part of the departmental pool.

Hard to believe, but this is the same location on 12 July 1995, the reference point being the mountain peak, Lose Hill, in the background. The industrial unit owned by Carbolite Ltd occupies the sidings site, blotting out the distant view of the station from this point. Class 158 DMU No 158787 sneaks past with the 13.40 Manchester Airport to Sheffield working. *John Spencer Gilks/Chris Milner*

GRINDLEFORD is near to the Derbyshire border, and this view on Saturday 11 June 1966 shows Class 25 No D7567 (25217) heading the 16.35 Sheffield Midland to Chinley local. Note the ground frame on the left, housed in a neat cabin, controlling the sidings.

Much remains the same on 12 July 1995 as Class 158 DMU No 158790 passes by on the 14.09 Sheffield to Manchester Airport. The signal box remains, but the sidings are now no longer used. Grindleford station remains open, served by ten trains each way on weekdays. The ridge of hills in the background is pierced by Totley Tunnel, 3 miles 950 yards long, the line emerging on the other side in South Yorkshire. The tunnel's western portal is only 100 yards from the end of Grindleford station platforms. Completed in 1893, the tunnel took six years to build. *Michael Mensing/Chris Milner*

136

Ambergate to Chesterfield

CLAY CROSS SOUTH JUNCTION (1): Looking now at the Midland Railway approach to Sheffield from Ambergate through Chesterfield, our first view is at Clay Cross South Junction on Saturday 10 July 1976, with Class 45 No 45142 (D83) coming off the line from Derby with a St Pancras to Sheffield working. The line going off to the left in the background is to Pye Bridge and Toton. Note the old coach body over to the left, which was a remnant from the Ashover Light Railway.

On 4 November 1995 virtually the complete layout is still intact, although the siding over to the right is now overgrown and not used, and the industrial backdrop is somewhat changed. Class 60 No 60031 *Ben Lui* heads back home to Teesside with a steel train from Shelton, Stoke-on-Trent. *Both Tom Heavyside*

CLAY CROSS SOUTH JUNCTION (2): Looking north on the same day, 10 July 1976. To the right are the sidings for Avenue Works, seen on the left, the bridge in the background being the rail access. Class 45 No 45142 returns south on the 18.03 Sheffield to St Pancras, passing class-mate No 45056 (D91) on a train of cement hoppers.

By Saturday 28 April 1990 the Avenue Works sidings have been lifted and nature is regaining its lost ground. The bridge in the background is still in situ, as it is today. Brightening up the scene is preserved Stanier '5MT' 4-6-0 No 44932 heading towards Derby on the return leg of the 'White Rose', its final destination being London Marylebone. The 'Black Five' had worked the special from Derby to Sheffield earlier in the day. *Both Tom Heavyside*

CHESTERFIELD (1), the second largest town in Derbyshire, was served by both the Great Central and Midland railways. The first line was opened between Derby and Masborough by the North Midland Railway on 11 May 1840, and through to Leeds on 30 June. Sheffield was ignored by George Stephenson, the line's engineer, as he wanted the easiest route to Leeds. When the direct route from Chesterfield to Sheffield opened on 1 February 1870, the Midland had overcome the route's problems, but not without some stiff gradients and having to construct the 1 mile 266 yard Bradway Tunnel. The original station at Chesterfield was rebuilt in 1964. Looking north away from the station in May 1959 Cricklewood-based Stanier '5MT' 4-6-0 No 45335 is seen heading south on an express for Derby, passing Toton's Stanier '8F' 2-8-0 No 48370 on a northbound freight. No 45335 was the first to be withdrawn in July 1965, with No 48370 going in November the following year, both from Annesley shed.

On 4 November 1995 Class 47 No 47741 *Resilient* (D1597) approaches Chesterfield on the 'Royal Scotsman' special from York to Frome. The sidings on the left of the previous photograph have gone, the area now covered with mature trees, and the bridge in the background has been rebuilt. *G. W. Sharpe/Tom Heavyside*

CHESTERFIELD (2): This is the view from the same footbridge, looking south towards the station in April 1959, the buildings being just visible in the background. Stanier '8F' 2-8-0 No 48062 heads north to Sheffield on a mineral train.

The view on 4 November 1995 shows that the main line has been slightly realigned over to the right, and the sidings and scrapyard have gone. Class 158 DMU No 158784 leaves on the 09.59 Norwich to Liverpool. Approaching the station is the 11.43 York to Poole headed by Class 47 No 47814 (D1919). *G. W. Sharpe/Tom Heavyside*

CHESTERFIELD (3): We are now looking back towards the footbridge used in the previous two sets of photographs on Saturday 10 July 1976. The famous crooked 228-foot 14th-century church spire of St Mary & All Saints looks down over the town; the use of unseasoned timber during its construction allowed the wooden frame to warp into the unique shape. Class 45 No 45115 (D81) draws away after its station stop with the 08.48 St Pancras to Sheffield.

Nineteen years later, on 4 November 1995, little has changed except the growth of trees, which is soon to obscure the sight of the spire. There are even discarded lengths of rail in the same spot over to the right of the photograph. Class 43 HST power car No 43060 *County of Leicestershire* heads the 06.20 Plymouth to Newcastle away from its 11.00 Chesterfield stop. *Both Tom Heavyside*

DRONFIELD is close to the Derbyshire border, and passing the station on Saturday 3 October 1959 on a southbound morning express is Derby-allocated Standard '5MT' 4-6-0 No 73157. This was one of the last Standard '5s' to be operational, withdrawal coming in May 1968 from Manchester Patricroft.

On 4 November 1995 the attractive stone bridge survives, as does the station's wooden fencing, and there is still an advertising board visible. The gas lighting has been replaced by electric standard lamps and once again the tree growth has increased. Class 141 DMU No 141114, based at Neville Hill, draws to a stop at 12.46 on the 11.10 from York to Chesterfield. *Michael Mensing/Tom Heavyside*

145

Great Central lines over Woodhead

The county of Derbyshire has a north-west thrust taking in Glossop and part of the area around Longdendale through which the Manchester to Sheffield route ran, which included Woodhead Tunnel. Eventually to become part of the Great Central Railway and then the LNER, it was electrified early on in British Railways days on the 1,500-volt DC system and opened for through traffic with electric traction on 3 June 1954. Its main purpose was heavy freight haulage, with a fleet of new locomotives built at Gorton Works and based on an earlier prototype built by the LNER in 1941. The prototype was named *Tommy* in June 1952, and the class became known as the 'Tommies', but officially under the TOPS system as Class 76. Fifty-seven were built and 14 equipped with train-heating boilers for passenger traffic. A further seven locomotives for passenger work were built during 1954, numbered 27000 to 27006 and designated Class 77; all seven were withdrawn in September 1968. Through passenger services over the line ceased on 5 January 1970, the last train from Manchester being the 18.40 departure and the return from Sheffield Victoria at 22.15, which actually left at 22.31. Both trains were hauled by No 26056.

MOTTRAM YARD was just inside Derbyshire at the Manchester end of the line. A train of eastbound MGR coal empties passes by hauled by Nos 76009 (26009) and 76036 (26036).

The passenger service remains from Manchester to Hadfield, taking in Glossop along the way, with a 30-minute frequency for most of the day. The original electrification catenary is still in use, with the voltage now standard at 25KV, the conversion from 1,500 volts DC taking place over the weekend of 8/9 December 1984. On Friday 20 October 1995 Class 305 EMU No 305510 passes the site of Mottram Yard on a Hadfield working. *Both Tom Heavyside*

147

GLOSSOP station is at the end of a 2-mile branch from the direct route to Hadfield. On Monday 1 May 1978 Class 506 1,500-volt DC EMU Nos 59603 + 59503 + 59403 awaits departure to Manchester Piccadilly. These units were introduced in 1954 for the local services on the line and were all withdrawn on conversion of the electric current in 1984.

In contrast to the 1978 view, by Thursday 2 November 1995 a new platform has been built on the opposite side of the line, and new electric masts have been installed. The site of the old platform is now part of a Co-op discount superstore. A link between the two views is the George Hotel in the background facing the station across the road. *Both Tom Heavyside*

DINTING RAILWAY CENTRE: Dinting was an ex-Great Central sub-shed to Gorton and was situated at the end of a short spur line to the west of the line between Dinting and Hadfield. Closure came in 1954, but it provided watering facilities for some time afterwards, the water tank surviving into preservation. The single-track engine shed and 10-acre site was purchased from British Railways in 1968 by Jack Warburton and the Dinting Steam Centre was developed. This included the building of a large three-road museum shed to house the growing collection, and this can be just seen over to the left behind the original building. Preserved Southern 'Schools' Class 4-4-0 No 30925 *Cheltenham*, minus coupling rods, was on show on Sunday 23 October 1977.

The sad sight at Dinting on 20 October 1995, a silent tribute to a preservation initiative that went wrong. The original shed building is now a listed structure and remains as it was, but the rest of the site is now completely cleared. The story of the Dinting Railway Centre's demise is a long and complicated one, but briefly it resulted from the landowner being unable to agree a renewed lease. Under the original agreement the site was leased at a nominal rent, but when this came up for renewal agreement was lacking. The Dinting Centre was therefore ordered to clear the site of all stock and fittings, and on Easter Monday, 16 April 1990, the last train ran in the Centre and dismantling of equipment began. All the stock had to be removed by 30 September, and a new home was found at the Keighley & Worth Valley Railway at Ingrow. *Both Tom Heavyside*

DINTING (1): Class 506 EMU Nos 59604 + 59504 + 59404 are seen at Dinting on a Hadfield-Glossop-Manchester Piccadilly working on Tuesday 1 January 1980. The track leading off to the left ran to the Dinting Railway Centre, and the removal of this link by British Rail during track realignment in 1989 created additional difficulties for the preservation group; the cost of reinstatement was £32,000. One survivor is the EMU which was saved from scrapping and is now at the Midland Railway Centre, Butterley.

On 12 July 1995 Class 305 EMU No 305503 passes on the 17.08 Hadfield to Manchester Piccadilly service. *Tom Heavyside/Chris Milner*

DINTING (2): Approaching the station on Saturday 14 April 1979 on a Hadfield to Manchester working is Class 506 DMU Nos 59602 + 59502 + 59402. In the background is Class 40 diesel No 40082 (D282) waiting to run into the station to take a return special to Guide Bridge, where Stanier '5MT' 4-6-0 No 5305 was to take over.

   The route is now single track with the former trackbed becoming overgrown with trees and shrubs. On 12 July 1995 EMU No 305503 passes on a Manchester to Hadfield local. *Tom Heavyside/Chris Milner*

HADFIELD: On Thursday 22 July 1976 Class 76 electric locomotives Nos 76010 (26010) and 76012 (26012) head a westbound coal train for Fiddlers Ferry.

Since closure of the Woodhead route Hadfield is now the end of the line. In this instance it was not possible to stand in exactly the same spot as the previous photographer because of the growth of trees over the old up line trackbed. On Thursday 2 November 1995 EMU No 30507 forms the 14.08 to Manchester. *Both Tom Heavyside*

TORSIDE, east of Hadfield, was where the B6105 road from Glossop crossed the railway on a level crossing. Class 76 No 76032 (26032) passes by with a westbound coal train and holds up the traffic on 22 July 1976. Torside Reservoir is in the background.

By Friday 20 October 1995 the road from Glossop has been realigned to ease the curves and the trackbed is now the Longdendale Trail, which in turn is part of the Trans-Pennine Trail. The Woodhead route officially closed from Monday 20 July 1981, but in reality Britain's first all-electric main line, and the first all-electric line to close, faded away in the early hours of Saturday 18 July. The last working was recorded at 05.10 at Woodhead powered by Nos 76014 (26014) and 76006 (26006), bringing to an end the last stretch of former Great Central main line. *Both Tom Heavyside*

WOODHEAD (1): About three-quarters of a mile west of Woodhead Tunnel on Thursday 9 June 1977, Class 76 No 76040 (26040) heads an eastbound mixed train, with the upper end of Woodhead Reservoir in the background.

The pylons remain and the stone wall on the left has been rebuilt and extended on 20 October 1995. Note the nearly empty reservoir, a reminder of the exceptional long dry summer of 1995. *Both Tom Heavyside*

WOODHEAD (2): Woodhead tunnel can be seen in the background of this view, recorded on Saturday 21 April 1979, of Class 76 No 76046 (26046) heading west from Sheffield on a Great Western Society special for Manchester.

In the 20 October 1995 view from the same spot, the Longdendale Trail nears the end of its route along the trackbed before taking its course over Woodhead Tunnel. Some new additional timber poles to the right of the picture now carry electric wires, but the link with the previous photograph has to be the pylons. *Both Tom Heavyside*

WOODHEAD (3): This 9 June 1977 view from the top of Woodhead Tunnel looking west along Longdendale shows two Class 76 locomotives approaching the tunnel entrance with an eastbound train of MGR empties.

The view on 20 October 1995 shows that many features remain, but apart from the absence of the track the main area of change is around the house on the left, with the railway buildings demolished and the house re-tiled. *Both Tom Heavyside*

WOODHEAD (4): Our last view in Derbyshire is of the western end of Woodhead Tunnel on 9 June 1977, with Class 76s No 76035 (26018) and 76033 (26033) on a westbound coal train. Over to the left can be seen the two original single-bore tunnels, which the new double-track tunnel replaced. Work on the new tunnel commenced in February 1949, the main contractors being Balfour Beatty & Co Ltd. The length of the tunnel, at 3 miles 66 yards, was 131 feet longer than the single-line tunnels and cost £4,250,000 to complete. It was ready for use in 1953 and opened for traffic on 3 June 1954.

On 2 November 1995 the tunnel entrance is securely sealed with iron gates and used by the National Grid. The stern warning on the notice attached to the gate says it all: 'DANGER OF DEATH, KEEP OUT'. *Both Tom Heavyside*

INDEX OF LOCATIONS